TZAVA'AT HARIVASH

TZAVA'AT HARIVASH

THE TESTAMENT
OF
RABBI ISRAEL BAAL SHEM TOV

English Translation
with Introduction, Notes and Commentary
by
JACOB IMMANUEL SCHOCHET

Published and Copyright by
KEHOT PUBLICATION SOCIETY
770 Eastern Parkway • Brooklyn, New York 11213

5758 • 1998

Copyright © 1998
by
J. Immanuel Schochet

Published by
Kehot Publication Society
770 Eastern Parkway / Brooklyn, New York 11213
(718) 774-4000 / FAX (718) 774-2718
e-mail: kehot@chabad.org

Orders Department:
291 Kingston Avenue / Brooklyn, New York 11213
(718) 778-0226 / FAX (718) 778-4148

Library of Congress Cataloging-in-Publication Data

Tsava'at ha-Rivash.   English.
The testament of Rabbi Israel Baal Shem Tov and rules of upright
conduct : consisting of instructions . . . heard from the holy mouth
of . . . Israel Baal Shem Tov . . . : and to those were added rules of upright conduct from the man of God . . . Dov Ber
of the community of Mezhirech.
Includes bibliographical references and index.
ISBN 0-8266-0399-8 (hard : alk.paper)
1.   Ba'al Shem Tov, ca 1700-1760—Will.   2. Wills, Ethical.
3. Hasidism.   I. Ba'al Shem Tov, ca.1700-1760.
II. DovBaer, of Mezhirech, d. 1772.   III. Title.
BJ1286.W6T7213   1998
296.3'6—dc21   98-12351
CIP

Printed in the United States of America

TESTAMENT
OF
RABBI ISRAEL BAAL SHEM TOV
AND
RULES OF UPRIGHT CONDUCT

CONSISTING OF INSTRUCTIONS, RULES OF PROPER CONDUCT, GREAT AND WONDROUS COUNSELS FOR THE SERVICE OF THE CREATOR, RELATING TO TORAH, PRAYER AND OTHER TRAITS, HEARD FROM THE HOLY MOUTH OF THE MAN OF GOD, THE HOLY LIGHT, OUR MASTER
RABBI ISRAEL BAAL SHEM TOV,
HIS MEMORY IS FOR A BLESSING, FOR THE LIFE OF THE WORLD TO COME; AND TO THESE WERE ADDED RULES OF UPRIGHT CONDUCT FROM THE MAN OF GOD, THE HOLY LIGHT, OUR MASTER
RABBI DOVBER
OF THE COMMUNITY OF MEZHIRECH

[Text of the original title-page]

TABLE OF CONTENTS

FOREWORD

In 1975, at the behest of the Lubavitcher Rebbe, R. Menachem M. Schneerson זי״ע, I published a new edition of *Tzava'at Harivash* with source-references, cross-references, brief commentaries, and other supplements. It is most gratifying that this has become the standard edition, and has already gone through four printings,[1] each with further additions.

In view of the present observance of the 300th anniversary of the birth of R. Israel Baal Shem Tov (18 Elul 5458-6 Sivan 5520), I acceded to many requests and translated *Tzava'at Harivash* into English. A number of teachings in this work had been translated before, appearing in various studies or anthologies of the Baal Shem Tov's teachings. This, however, is the first translation of the complete text.

This English rendition follows my original Hebrew edition in the division of the text into separate sections.[2] Any translation is of itself an interpretation, for which the translator must assume full responsibility. Even so, I added to each segment brief comments and explanations. These include,

---

1. A fifth edition, with corrections and further additions, is presently in print and will appear shortly.
2. The only divergence is in joining sections 2 and 3, 5 and 6, 7 and 8, 13 and 14, 17 to 19, 26 and 27, 60 and 61, 78 and 79, 82 and 83, and 126 and 127. Careful review of the material convinced me that these combinations are more appropriate than my original division. Also, in line with the nature of the contents as instructions for "proper conduct and practices," the text's general usage of third person was changed (in most cases) to second person.

where it was felt to be necessary or helpful, citations of earlier sources that elucidate the contents or indicate authoritative roots for the ideas stated.[3] An extensive introduction discusses the literary origin of *Tzava'at Harivash*, the central themes that appear in it, and the impact of its publication.

Chassidism made it possible that everyone, from scholar to simpleton, be able to taste from the Tree of Life of *pnimiyut haTorah*, the inner dimension of the Torah, the mystical tradition of Judaism. Indeed, the Baal Shem Tov records in a famous letter addressed to his brother in-law, the renowned R. Abraham Gershon of Kitov, that it was revealed to him that the Messianic redemption will follow when his teachings "will become renowned and will be revealed throughout the world, and 'your wellsprings will be dispersed *chutzah* (abroad; externally)' . . . for then the *kelipot* (aspects of evil) will perish and it will be a time of propitiousness and deliverance."

Thus it is our prayerful hope that this work be not only a worthy noting of the present anniversary, but also be conducive in bringing the inspiration of the Baal Shem Tov and Chassidism to an ever-widening audience. This will surely hasten the promise made to the Baal Shem Tov of bringing about the Messianic redemption when "the earth shall be full with the knowledge of God as the waters cover the sea" (Isaiah 11:9) "and they shall teach no more every man his neighbor and every man his brother saying, 'Know God,' for they shall *all* know Me, from the least of them unto the greatest of them" (Jeremiah 31:33).

J. Immanuel Schochet

Toronto, Ont., 11 Nissan, 5758

---

3. In view of the numerous references to *Maggid Devarav Leya'akov* the appendix offers a comparative table of the principal editions currently in use.

INTRODUCTION

I

THE LITERARY ORIGIN OF *TZAVA'AT HARIVASH*

Tzava'at Harivash is one of the earliest Chassidic texts to be published. Its first edition appeared in 1792 or 1793 (no date is mentioned). It was preceded only by R. Ya'akov Yossef of Polnoy's *Toldot Ya'akov Yossef* (1780), *Ben Porat Yossef* (1781) and *Tzafnat Pane'ach* (1782); and R. Dov Ber of Mezhirech's *Maggid Devarav Leya'akov*, also known as *Likkutei Amarim* (1781; second edition with supplements 1784; third edition 1792), and *Likkutim Yekarim*, which incorporates R. Meshulam Feivish of Zborez' *Yosher Divrei Emet* (1792).

Tzava'at Harivash is an anthology of teachings and instructions attributed to the Baal Shem Tov and his successor, R. Dov Ber, the Maggid of Mezhirech. It is identical in form and style to *Maggid Devarav Leya'akov* and *Likkutim Yekarim*. To a great extent it is identical to these also in content: the major part of our text appeared already in *Likkutim Yekarim*, and a few additional sections in *Maggid Devarav Leya'akov*. In fact, all of its contents can be found in anthologies of the Maggid's teachings, though some of these were published later: all but six[1] of its 143[2] sections appear in *Or Ha'emet* (first published in 1899); seventy-four appear in *Likkutim Yekarim*; forty-three appear in the *Likkutei Amarim* attributed to R. Menachem Mendel of Vitebsk (first published in 1911); thirty-three in *Or Torah* (first published in 1804); and three (and with some

---

1. Sections 102, 123, 125, and 141-143.
2. Actually there are only 141 sections: sect. 57 is a duplication of sect. 42, and sect. 113 is a duplication of sect. 51. Note also that sect. 35 is a variation on 42, and sect. 97 is essentially a brief version of sect. 62.

variations another five) in *Maggid Devarav Leya'akov*. Some appear also in *Kitvei Kodesh* (1884) and in *Shemu'ah Tovah* (1938). These duplications beg consideration to determine the origin of *Tzava'at Harivash*.

The original title-page reads as follows:

> *"Book of the Testament of Rabbi Israel Baal Shem and Hanhagot Yesharot (rules of upright conduct)*—that was found in the valise of ... Rabbi Isaiah, Head of the Rabbinic Court and Head of the Academy of the holy community of Yanov—which consists of *tzava'ot* (instructions), rules of proper conduct, great and wondrous counsels for the service of the Creator relating to Torah and prayer and other traits, heard from the holy mouth of the Man of God, the Holy Light, our Master Rabbi Israel Baal Shem Tov, his memory is for a blessing, for the life of the world-to-come. To these were added *Hanhagot Yesharot* from the Man of God, the Holy Light, our Master Rabbi Dov Ber of the community of Mezhirech."

In the text itself, nineteen sayings appear with the name of the Baal Shem Tov.[3] In other early sources we find attributions to the Baal Shem Tov for another five teachings.[4] Explicit attribution to the Maggid appears in our text only once.[5]

---

3. Sect. 1, 10, 17-19, 31, 41, 75, 76, 91-93, 96, 100, 101-b, 106, 109, 120 and 124.
4. Sect. 47, 64-65, 69 and 73; see my notes on these sections in the Hebrew edition.
5. Sect. 101. Some have suggested that the heading preceding this section may be meant for all the sections from there on. This appears rather untenable, because it would create the assumption that everything up to there is from the Baal Shem Tov, to the exclusion of the rest, when in fact both parts are of the same nature.

It is not known who compiled *Tzava'at Harivash*. It is also not known who compiled *Likkutim Yekarim*[6] and *Or Torah*.[7] *Maggid Devarav Leya'akov* was edited by R. Shelomoh of Lutzk, a disciple and relative of the Maggid, from manuscripts written by others.[8] *Or Ha'emet* was printed from a manuscript of R. Levi Yitzchak of Berdichev, as was also *Shemu'ah Tovah*.[9] *Likkutei Amarim* (Vitebsk) was printed from a manuscript found among the possessions of R. Menachem Mendel of Vitebsk and erroneously attributed to him by the publishers. Its contents are identical to a manuscript that was in the possession of R. Shemuel Shmelka of Nikolsburg, the title-page of which reads: "*Likkutei Amarim* of the saintly rabbi, the famous Holy Light, the Maggid of the holy community of Mezhirech, our Master R. Dov Ber ... compiled ... by his disciple ... R. Shmelka, the rabbi of the holy community of the capital Nikolsburg."[10] *Kitvei Kodesh* was printed from manuscripts owned by R. Israel of Kozienice, another disciple of the Maggid.[11]

---

6. Some suspect that it is R. Meshulam Feivish of Zborez because he mentions manuscripts of the Maggid in his possession and his own *Yosher Divrei Emet* was incorporated in *Likkutim Yekarim*. As stated below, it is indeed most likely that *Likkutim Yekarim* was published from his manuscripts, but not necessarily by him.

7. Its title-page mentions merely that this work was published from manuscripts in the possession of, and verified by, R. Yeshayah of Donavitz.

8. See below the quotation from the introduction to *Maggid Devarav Leya'akov*.

9. See the publishers' forewords to these works.

10. Photostats of this manuscript's title-page, and 2 pages of its contents, appear in *Torat Hamaggid Mimezhirech*, pp. [7-9].

11. See the publisher's foreword. *Darkei Yesharim—Hanhagot Yesharot*, attributed to R. Menachem Mendel of Premishlan [Przemysl] (first published around 1800; see A. M. Haberman's bibliographical list in *Sefer Habesht*, Jerusalem 1960, p. 46ff.) is not included in our list. Indeed, 27 sections of *Tzava'at Harivash* appear there as well, but the number and type of its variations and additions necessitate a separate study of its origin.

All these works contain teachings that appear in the others. Most duplications are generally identical. Some appear partially, or in brief versions, in one text, and completely, or more elaborately, in another, but otherwise there are but minor variations.

Tzava'at Harivash is the only one of these anthologies that does not contain anything original, i.e., anything that is not found in the others. It is noteworthy that it contains two sections that I found only in *Likkutim Yekarim*,[12] two that I found only in *Or Torah*,[13] and ten that I found only in *Or Ha'emet*.[14] Moreover, there are significant omissions in some of its versions, including one[15] that leaves its rendition incomplete. This raises some questions about its literary origin. A closer study of the sources, however, provides the answer.

The first in the series of publications of the Maggid's teachings is, as noted above, *Maggid Devarav Leya'akov*. Its editor, R. Shelomoh of Lutzk, relates in his detailed introduction that a number of manuscripts of the Maggid's teachings circulated in his time, arbitrary anthologies without any order or system and (at least some) copied from one another. Generally they were full of errors, confusion and omissions that would require total re-writing which, he complains, would have been very difficult for him. Fortunately, however, he came into possession of

> "a number of manuscripts written by various people, and especially copied from the handwriting of R. Ze'ev Wolf of Greater Horodna in Lithuania, and edited by

---

12. Sect. 141 and 143. (Only half of sect. 143 was printed in *Tzava'at Harivash*.)
13. Sect. 102 and 123. *Maggid Devarav Leya'akov*, sect. 58, has a brief passage with great similarity to sect. 123 and most likely is taken from the same discourse.
14. Sect. 15-16, 51 (duplicated in sect. 113), 76, 97, 99-101a-b and 115. (Only part of sect. 101-b was printed in *Tzava'at Harivash*.)
15. Sect. 143, as noted above, note 12.

him. I found [in them] ... delightful discourses that I still remember, but it was impossible for me to re-write them and to arrange them in orderly fashion."

R. Shelomoh published these manuscripts unaltered as the book *Maggid Devarav Leya'akov*.

R. Meshulam Feivish of Zborez writes in the introduction to *Yosher Divrei Emet*[16] (which was incorporated in *Likkutim Yekarim*) that he merited to attend to the Maggid and later on (after the Maggid's passing) obtained "sacred writings of his holy words." He mentions these manuscripts several times, and all his references can be found in *Likkutim Yekarim*.[17] It is safe to assume that the publisher of *Likkutim Yekarim* used his manuscript(s) to publish that work, as appears also from the fact that his *Yosher Divrei Emet* was incorporated therein.

Thus we find a series of manuscripts containing identical writings in the hands of R. Ze'ev Wolf of Horodna and R. Shelomoh of Lutzk (*Maggid Devarav Leya'akov*), R. Meshulam Feivish of Zborez (*Likkutim Yekarim*), R. Yeshayah of Dono-vitz (*Or Torah*), R. Levi Yitzchak of Berdichev (*Or Ha'emet, Shemu'ah Tovah*), R. Israel of Kozinice (*Kitvei Kodesh*), R. Men-achem Mendel of Vitebsk (*Likkutei Amarim*), R. Shemu'el Shmelka of Nikolsburg (*Likkutei Amarim*-MS), and R. Yesha-yah of Yanov (*Tzava'at Harivash*), aside of the anonymous manuscripts mentioned by R. Shelomoh of Lutzk. The identi-cal contents clearly indicate that all of these must have had a singular source. The differences between them (additional materials, omissions, textual variations and so forth) can be accounted for by some having more or less complete manu-

16. Written in 5777, as noted by the author there, ch. 1 (p. 110a) and ch. 14 (p. 117a)

17. See there ch. 15 (pp. 117b and 118a), ch. 17 (p. 118b), ch. 19 (p. 120a), ch. 41 (p. 134a), ch. 42 (p. 134a) and ch. 56 (p. 142b).

scripts, and the many hands of copyists until the respective manuscript came into the hands of the rabbis.[18]

Tzava'at Harivash differs from all these other works in one important respect: it is not simply a copy of one or more of these manuscripts, but an edited selection of teachings with one theme, as indicated in the title-page. Its editor selected passages that would form a manual for religious ethics.

The manuscripts used by the anonymous editor were not the best. They were obviously defective, as appears from significant omissions in our text which otherwise make no sense at all. These omissions are of two kinds: a)there is much more material in the other works that fits the theme of *Tzava'at Harivash* and would surely have been included if available to the editor; and b)section 143, as mentioned above, was left incomplete.

This analysis of the origin of *Tzava'at Harivash*[19] is supported by the testimony of an authoritative contemporary, R. Schneur Zalman of Liadi, a principal disciple of the Maggid. He verifies the absolute authenticity of our book's contents, but also comments that

> "it is not at all [the Baal Shem Tov's] last will, and he did not decree anything before his passing. [Its contents] are but collections of his pure sayings that were gathered 'gleanings upon gleanings,' and [the compil-

---

18. These manuscripts were already written and copied, and circulated widely to the point of reaching also the hands of the adversaries of Chassidism, in the life-time of the Maggid. The wording in the criticism against the Chassidic emphasis on joy and condemnation of melancholy that appeared in *Zemir Aritzim Vechorbot Tzurim* (ed. Wilensky, p. 38), published in 1772 (thus during the life-time of the Maggid), clearly indicates that the author had a manuscript containing section sect. 46 in *Tzava'at Harivash*.

19. See also Z. Gries, "Arichat *Tzava'at Harivash*," *Kiryat Sefer*, vol. 52, Jerusalem 1977, pp. 187-210; and of related interest, his "*Safrut Hahanhagot Hachassidit*," *Zion* 46:4, Jerusalem 1981, pp. 198-305.

ers] were unable to phrase it exactly... for the Baal Shem Tov, of blessed memory, would deliver his Torah-discourses in Yiddish, and not in the sacred tongue (Hebrew)."[20]

"Gleanings upon gleanings," a Talmudic expression (*Ta'anit* 6b), means that our editor's manuscript had passed through various stages: copies were made from the original manuscript(s) of an anthology of the Baal Shem Tov and the Maggid's teachings, and later copyists omitted some parts (and perhaps added others from different manuscripts) until some late copy or copies came into the hands of our editor from which he made his selection that comprises our text.

II
BASIC CONCEPTS IN TZAVA'AT HARIVASH

Deveikut

The central theme in *Tzava'at Harivash*, not surprisingly, is the ultimate of Chassidism's religious values: *deveikut*, attachment or cleaving unto God. It implies constant communion with God, a vivid and overwhelming consciousness of the Omnipresent as the sole true reality. It is an all-comprehensive principle, that relates not only to prayer[21] and Torah-study[22], but also to man's mundane engagements in the daily life.[23] Its pursuit enables man to achieve the level of equanimity by means of which he transcends worldly thoughts and con-

---

20. *Tanya, Igeret Hakodesh*, sect. 25, pp. 138a-b and 141a.
21. See below, note 27.
22. See sect. 29-30.
23. See sect. 3, 30, 81, 84, 101 and 136.

cerns.[24] Little wonder, then, that it is a recurring theme throughout our text.[25]

Prayer

The most frequently mentioned concept in *Tzava'at Harivash* is prayer. It is the subject of over 40 sections. The predominance of this theme is readily understood in view of the Chassidic emphasis on prayer. For prayer is the most direct and most common occasion for *deveikut*. It is also universal, relating to the common folks no less than to the saint and scholar. Every individual, without distinction, can and must engage in this form of communion with God. Moreover, R. Isaac Luria, the supreme authority of Jewish mysticism, ruled: in the present era, the period of *ikvot Meshichah* ("on the heels of Mashiach," i.e., the period just prior to the Messianic redemption) the primary service of God, and the primary *birur* (refinement and correction of the world that leads to the Messianic redemption), is expressly through prayer, though Torah-study is in principle superior to worship.[26] Thus we are told that the Baal Shem Tov merited his unique attainment of spiritual perfection and his revelations of supernal matters by virtue of his prayers with great *kavanah* (devotion), and not by virtue of his extensive study of the Talmud and the codifiers.[27] *Tzava'at Harivash* is then replete with emphasis on the significance of prayer and guidance for proper prayer and worship:

---

24. See sect. 10, and see below, *s.v.* Religious Ethics in Daily Life.
25. In addition to the cited references see also sect. 12, 31, 38-39, 63, 80, 82, 111 and 135.
26. *Peri Eitz Chayim, Sha'ar Hatefilah*, ch. 7; and cf. *Eitz Chayim* 39:1-2 and 47:6. See *Tanya, Kuntres Acharon*, sect. 4 (p. 155aff.) and sect. 8 (p. 162a).
27. Sect. 41.

Prayer is union with the *Shechinah*.[28] In, and through, prayer, one is to attain the level of *deveikut*,[29] a *deveikut* that will then extend beyond the prayers into the daily activities.[30] Thus one must pray with all one's strength[31] to the extent that the words themselves become alight,[32] and it should be with joy[33] and *hitlahavut* (fervor; ecstasy).[34] Proper *kavanah* is possible only with personal exertion.[35] Initially this may necessitate to pray out loud, bodily movements (swaying), and reading from the prayer-book, to stimulate *kavanah*.[36] The ideal prayer, though, the prayer that is altogether from within, is inaudible and immobile.[37]

The focus in prayer is not to be on personal gains, but to serve God and fulfill His Will.[38] This will also avoid being perturbed by alien thoughts in prayer.[39] Unavoidable disturbances from without are Providential, to spur man to greater effort on concentration and devotion.[40]

The attainment of the proper state requires gradual stages of ascent.[41] Special effort must be made at the very beginning and that at least part of the prayer is in proper fashion.[42] One is not to be discouraged when it seems difficult to concentrate

---

28. Sect. 68.
29. Sect. 32-33, 35, 37, 40, 42, 57-59, 61, 67-70, 105, 123 and 136.
30. Sect. 37.
31. Sect. 33-35, 58, 75 and 108.
32. Sect. 75.
33. Sect. 107-108.
34. Sect. 118.
35. Sect. 60-61 and 72.
36. Sect. 40, 58-59, 68 and 104-105.
37. Sect. 33, 58-59, 68 and 104-105.
38. Sect. 4, 62, 73, 84, 97 and 123.
39. Sect. 62 and 97.
40. Sect. 120.
41. Sect. 32, 61 and 143.
42. Sect. 19 and 61.

properly: strengthen yourself and make every effort to overcome the barriers, entreat God for His assistance and you will succeed.[43]

Torah-Study

The emphasis on *deveikut* and prayer is not to belittle the significance and central role of Torah-study. Torah-study is all-important. It furbishes the soul[44] and is the essential antidote to the temptations of the *yetzer hara* (inclination to evil).[45] It must be pursued with all one's strength and energy.[46] "God and the Torah are entirely one;" the Torah is God's "garment."[47] Torah-study, therefore, relates man directly with God.[48] Thus it must be done with joy, awe and love,[49] which also offers the benefit of reducing alien thoughts.[50]

When studying one must concentrate on the subject-matter, to understand it properly.[51] To be sure, this means that one cannot simultaneously concentrate on the ultimate goal of *deveikut*.[52] Nonetheless, one must study because (a)failure to do so leads to cessation of *deveikut*;[53] (b)by virtue of proper Torah-study one will be duly attached to Godliness;[54] and (c)the time spent on Torah-study is certainly not inferior to the states when conscious *deveikut* is precluded, as when

---

43. Sect. 58, 60-61 and 72.
44. Sect. 29.
45. Sect. 38.
46. Sect. 33-34, 51 and 113. See also the notes on sect. 117.
47. Sect. 111.
48. Sect. 54 and 119.
49. Sect. 51, 113 and 119.
50. Sect. 51 and 113.
51. Sect. 30.
52. Sect. 29-30.
53. Sect. 29.
54. Sect. 30.

sleeping or the mind "falls."[55] Indeed, failure to study Torah is a principal cause of all spiritual harms and defects.[56]

Even so, when studying Torah one must be aware that it is God's Torah, thus "before Whom you are learning"[57] and that God Himself is "concentrated, as it were, in the four cubits of *Halachah*."[58] Thus every so often one ought to interrupt the study to remind himself thereof and to attach himself unto God.[59] In this context one is not to limit the curriculum to theoretical studies of the Talmud and its commentaries, but also include works of religious ethics that further fear of Heaven[60]—and to study these every day[61]—as well as the codes of law in order to know the proper observance of the law.[62]

Mitzvot

One must be very careful with the fulfillment of the *mitzvot* (religious obligations). Torah-study, prayer and the other *mitzvot* must always be observed with the appropriate devotions, *lishmah* (for their own sake as Divine precepts), "for the sake of Heaven," i.e., to serve God and to carry out His Will. They must be devoid of any ulterior motives, whether these be material or spiritual.[63]

Even so, the lack of ideal intent can never be an excuse for not carrying out any of these obligations.[64] There is an objec-

---

55. Sect. 29.
56. Sect. 121.
57. Sect. 54.
58. Sect. 119.
59. Sect. 29.
60. Sect. 117.
61. Sect. 1.
62. Sect. 117.
63. Sect. 2-3, 11, 20, 43-44, 46-47, 73, 84, 94-95, 122-123, 101, 116 and 127.
64. Sect. 55 and 126.

tive validity and value in the very act of a *mitzvah*;[65] thus do as many *mitzvot* as you can and eventually you will perform them in proper fashion.[66] The underlying principle of obedience to do God's Will assures observance of all *mitzvot*, without distinction whether they are major or minor, for all are equally Divine precepts that must be observed carefully.[67] It is very important that not a single day pass by without performing at least one *mitzvah*,[68] and that the *mitzvot* be done with alacrity and zeal.[69]

Joy

Chassidism is known for its emphasis on joy and a happy frame of mind, and its categorical rejection of sadness and melancholy. This, too, is a dominant theme in *Tzava'at Harivash*:

Sadness is a repugnant character-trait,[70] a barrier to the service of God.[71] It is a typical objective of the *yetzer hara* who pretends to seek man's religious self-improvement by harping on one's real or imagined shortcomings and failures in order to generate a sense of worthlessness and hopelessness.[72] Thus one must be extremely cautious to recognize this ruse of the *yetzer hara* and not fall into his trap.[73]

Man must be disturbed and upset by wrong-doing and defects. The need of penitence, however, must be in context

---

65. Sect. 126.
66. Sect. 55.
67. Sect. 1, 17 and 122.
68. Sect. 1 and 17.
69. Sect. 20 and 116.
70. Sect. 46.
71. Sect. 44 and 46.
72. *Ibid.*
73. *Ibid.*

of correcting these deficiencies and enhancing attachment to God and observance of Torah and *mitzvot*. Self-improvement and self-correction may even necessitate fasting and self-mortification,[74] with care that it be without ulterior motives,[75] notwithstanding the fact that, generally speaking, fasting and self-affliction should be avoided because they cause feelings of sadness and depression.[76]

True *teshuvah* (return to God) and authentic worship focus on God and not oneself. This implies a joyful pursuit of the service of prayer and the observance of the *mitzvot*.[77] Thus weeping is bad, unless it is an expression of joy (or in the context of *teshuvah* at the appropriate times, or when beseeching God in momentary occasions of dire distress).[78] One must be happy at all times,[79] especially when serving God,[80] with prayer[81] and Torah-study.[82]

Even so, the constant joy must be tempered by an accompanying awe and fear of God.[83] Love and fear of God must go hand in hand, lest the one turn into carelessness and the other into depression.[84]

---

74. Sect. 56 and 78-79.
75. Sect. 43 and 77.
76. Sect. 56.
77. Sect. 44 and 46.
78. Sect. 45 and 107.
79. Sect. 15, 44-46 and 137.
80. Sect. 44-45.
81. Sect. 107-108.
82. Sect. 51 and 119.
83. Sect. 110.
84. Sect. 110 and 128.

Religious Ethics in Daily Life

Service of God is not limited to rituals like Torah, *mitzvot* and prayer. God is to be served in all possible ways.[85] Thus "know and acknowledge God in all your ways," even in your mundane engagements, i.e., in all involvements with the physical reality of man.[86]

The materiality of the body is an obstructing barrier to the soul[87] and its mundane desires must be disregarded and despised.[88] At the same time, however, the soul cannot function on earth without the body. Thus one must safeguard physical health, for illness of the body weakens the soul.[89] One must eat, drink and sleep to maintain health, to be strengthened for the Divine service.[90]

Moreover, all physical entities contain holy sparks which are the very vitality sustaining them. The fact that physical objects come your way is a Providential indication that their sparks relate to your soul. Your proper use of these items, in context of the Divine service, redeems and elevates these sparks, thus actualizing the intended purpose of the items.[91] Thus matter itself is sublimated to holiness. Indeed, *chomer,* matter and physical reality, becomes a direct cause of spiritual gain and achievement.[92]

One must be careful, though, not to be drawn after the mundane. It is only a means toward an end, and not an end in itself. Thus do not eat or drink excessively, but only to the ex-

---

85. Sect. 3.
86. Sect. 94.
87. Sect. 80.
88. Sect. 6 and 9.
89. Sect. 106.
90. Sect. 5 and 22.
91. Sect. 31, 109, 127 and 141.
92. Sect. 100.

tent of maintaining your health.[93] Indulgence leads to spiritual downfall.[94] Likewise, all personal transactions must be conducted with *da'at,* knowledge and forethought.[95] Even the intent viewing of the mundane desensitizes and brings crudity upon oneself.[96]

Man's thought must always be focused on God, on the spiritual reality. Involvements with the mundane may be neccessary, but only as temporary digressions. They are like momentary departures from your true home with the mind set on returning as soon as possible.[97]

The ideal attitude is one of equanimity: total indifference to personal delight or pleasure, and to other peoples' praise or blame.[98] This is achieved by constant attachment to God, implicit belief in Divine Providence, and total submission to God.[99]

In this scheme there is no room for sanctimonious self-satisfaction.[100] Equanimity and spiritual growth require self-negation.[101] Sincere humility, self-deprecation, is the very sign of the true servant of God.[102] When preoccupied with the service of God there is simply no time to think of self, and for pride or other evil character-traits to arise.[103] Self-esteem and arrogance is a most serious offense, the root of all evil, gener-

---

93. Sect. 5.
94. Sect. 121 and 131.
95. Sect. 98; and see also sect. 101.
96. Sect. 5 and 121.
97. Sect. 84.
98. Sect. 2, 6, 10, 49, 84 and 127.
99. Sect. 2 and 10.
100. Sect. 12 and 77.
101. Sect. 53.
102. Sect. 114.
103. Sect. 52.

ates alien thoughts, and separates man from God.[104] This applies especially to the self-satisfaction from spiritual activities and assumed achievements.[105]

These are some of the central themes in this work. For others, the reader is directed to the index, especially for the extensive treatments of "thought" and "speech." One more subject, however, does require further elaboration:

Sublimation of Alien Thoughts and *Yeridah Tzorech Aliyah*

A. The concept of *machshavah zara* is a frequent theme in *Tzava'at Harivash*. The literal meaning of this term is "alien thought." It is often translated as "evil, lustful or sinful thought," but that rendition is too restrictive. It includes any thought or feeling that is inappropriate to the occasion, whether it be sinful *per se* or not, thus we used the literal meaning throughout.

Man is often beset by such thoughts or feelings. Their intrusion is especially disturbing when it occurs during prayer or other religious practices. If this should happen, the general advice is *hessech hada'at*, diversion of attention that would result in the immediate dismissal of the inappropriate thoughts.[106] In *Tzava'at Harivash*, however, as well as in other early Chassidic works, we find another approach:

Man's feelings or emotive traits consist of seven categories, corresponding to the Divine attributes known by their Kabbalistic term as the *Sefirot*: 1) love of something, marked by attraction, and also manifesting itself in terms of kindness; 2) fear of something, marked by repulsion, and also manifesting

---

104. Sect. 62, 92 and 97.
105. Sect. 74, 122, 124 and 131.
106. See below, notes 127-128.

itself in terms of severity or strictness; 3)recognition of an inherent quality of status, such as beauty or some achievement, manifesting itself in praise or admiration; 4) the trait to endure, prevail or conquer; 5) the trait of acknowledgment, or of a restraining splendor; 6) the trait of bonding, of establishing a relationship; and 7) the trait of governance in the sense of applying the other traits. (The seventh differs from the others in that it is more passive, dependent on the others, rather than active.)[107]

These seven traits are analogous to the *Sefirot* because they are a reflection, worldly counter-parts, as it were, of the Divine attributes, and rooted therein. For ultimately all things are rooted in the Divine. The *Sefirot*, however, are altogether holy and good. The human traits, on the other hand, are like man himself: they can be holy and good or manifest themselves as the very opposite. Thus there is a "good love" and a "good fear," relating to that which ought to be loved or feared, and there is the fall to "bad love" (illicit love, or love of sins) and to "bad fear" (inappropriate fear, or hatred). There is the "good admiration" of the holy and sublime, and there is the fall to "bad admiration" as in pride and self-esteem; and so forth.[108]

The concept of the "sublimation of alien thoughts or feelings" is based on this contrariety. The alien thought is bad. Its category, however, has a good side and a bad side. Sublimation would then mean to trace the bad thought to its good source and transform it into a good thought. For example, mundane beauty is rooted in, and a pale reflection of, the source of all beauty on high, in Divinity. Why, then, would one pursue the mere reflection when he can have the all-inclusive source? The inappropriate love of, and attraction to-

---

107. Sect. 89.
108. *Ibid.*

ward, something mundane, something that is transient and illusory, thus is to be traced to the ultimate source of love and attraction in holiness and transformed into a love and pursuit of the holy. The same applies to all other categories of thought and feeling.[109] That is how the alien thoughts are elevated and sublimated to become holy, and in the process elevate man himself as well: there was a momentary descent to the depth of the alien thought, culminating in an ascent to a level transcending one's original status.[110]

This concept has nothing to do with the Sabbatean heresy of engaging in forbidden activities to "elevate" the forbidden and impure. To be sure, the evil and forbidden, too, contain holy sparks that enable them to exist. Those sparks, however, can be released and redeemed only by relating to those objects as prescribed by the Torah, i.e., by rejecting them. The rejection of evil releases the sparks, thus deprives evil of its source of vitality, and that is how evil is subdued and removed.[111] All the best intentions in using them in ways that violate Torah-law will not consecrate or elevate them. On the contrary: any prohibited contact with, or use of, forbidden objects, or engagement in illicit activities, infuses them with greater vitality, thus empowers and enhances the forces of evil and impurity.[112]

Chassidic works present the principle of sublimating alien thoughts, but they do so with the warning that it is hazardous. There is a real danger that engaging in sublimation may be counter-productive and lead astray. It requires Divine assis-

---

109. Sect. 14, 22, 87, 90, 101-b, 120 and 127.
110. Sect. 64. [A proper understanding of the Chassidic concept of sublimating "alien thoughts and feelings" requires consideration of two crucial explanations, both attributed to the Baal Shem Tov: *Ben Porat Yossef, Vayechi,* p. 85a (and see there also p. 85b), and *Me'or Einayim, Va'etchanan,* p. 62b-c.]
111. Sect. 9.
112. Sect. 87, 90 and 124.

tance as a safeguard.[113] Only the enthused person, one praying with *hitlahavut,* is to engage in sublimation. All others must put their efforts into praying more intensely.[114]

These qualifications are reiterated more emphatically in other texts. The Baal Shem Tov states that the sublimation of alien or extraneous thoughts requires *hachna'ah, havdalah* and *hamtakah. Hamtakah,* the "sweetening" of the forbidden thoughts (i.e., their sublimation to holiness), can follow only after an initial *hachna'ah,* "subduing" with total divestment of self or any personal attachment, and *havdalah,* their complete separation from the *kelipot,* i.e., a separation from any link with the realm of evil. These initial steps are earmarked by a profound sense of dread, that the person is overcome by a gripping fear of God.[115]

In at least two other instances we find that the Baal Shem Tov adds cautionary qualifications to this principle. In one[116] he adds the verse "It is the glory of God to conceal the matter" (Proverbs 25:2), suggesting that this is an esoteric teaching that is not meant for the average person lest it be abused.[117] In the other[118] he adds the conclusion: "To dwell on this at length involves danger, and the wise will be silent!"

R. Yaakov Yossef of Polnoy, who recorded these teachings of his master, the Baal Shem Tov, is more explicit. After explaining the principle of sublimating evil and alien thoughts in context of Divine Providence, he notes: "Sometimes, how-

---

113. Sect. 140.

114. Sect. 87.

115. *Toldot Ya'akov Yossef,* Addenda, par. 13, 15 and 16 (p. 729b-d), and see there also par. 25 (p. 731b); *Ben Porat Yossef,* end of *Lech Lecha* (p. 29c). All this is cited in *Keter Shem Tov,* sect. 28, 160, 163 and 302, see there. Note also *Maggid Devarav Leya'akov,* sect. 228; and *Or Torah,* sect. 277.

116. *Toldot Ya'akov Yossef,* Eikev: I (p. 629a).

117. *Cf. Shabbat* 153b.

118. *Toldot Ya'akov Yossef,* Eikev: III (p. 632a).

ever, [this] thought must be repelled. You may ask, 'how will I know which thought must be repelled, and which is to be brought near and elevated?' [The answer is:] Man must consider [the following]. If the means to correct and elevate the alien thought will arise in your mind immediately as it comes to you, then see to bring it near and sublimate it. If, however, the means to correct it will not arise immediately in the mind, it may be assumed that [the alien thought] came about to disturb man in his prayer and to confuse his thought. It is then permissible to repel that thought, for 'if one comes to slay you, forestall [by slaying him]' (*Sanhedrin* 72a)."[119]

R. Dov Ber, the Maggid of Mezhirech and successor of the Baal Shem Tov, too, relates the principle of sublimation to the premise of Divine Providence. In one lengthy discussion[120] he traces the occurrence of alien thoughts to one of two sources: a)they may be a reflection of the person's evil deeds in the past, which now offer an opportunity to be corrected; or b)they are rooted in the cosmic "breaking of the vessels," independent of the individual. The latter, however, relates only to a *tzadik* who is to elevate them to their spiritual source. In either case, however, they entered the mind beyond the person's control. One must never introduce them on his own: "If one will say, 'I shall intentionally meditate to bring about [an alien thought of] love so that [I may] elevate it,' of him it is said 'That you awaken not, nor stir up, love, until it please.' (Song 2:7; 3:5) Our sages, of blessed memory said of this that 'he who wilfully excites himself shall be under the ban' (*Nidah* 13b), that is, he is distanced from God. He thinks that he is close, but in truth he is removed."

---

119. *Ben Porat Yossef, Toldot*, p. 50c, cited in *Keter Shem Tov*, sect. 39.
120. *Maggid Devarav Leya'akov*, sect. 213; also in *Likkutim Yekarim*, sect. 98, and *Or Torah*, sect. 115 (which has significant variants); cited (partially) in *Keter Shem Tov*, sect. 207.

This distinction appears again in the Maggid's interpretation of "*Ikvotecha* (Your footsteps; lit. 'the mark of your heels') were not known" (Psalms 77:20): *eikev* (heel) refers to the lowest levels. Sometimes, however, these can ascend, as in the case of an alien thought in the midst of prayer. This, however, is an aspect of *hora'at sha'ah* (a temporary decision or dispensation). The term *sha'ah* is an expression of "let them not pay attention to false words" (Exodus 5:9; see Rashi there). This means that in the case of sublimation there was a time when that thing had to be elevated, analogous to Elijah on Mount Carmel: he brought offerings there in spite of the prohibition of sacrificing on *bamot* (altars outside the Holy Temple in Jerusalem),[121] because he had to elevate the whole generation that worshipped idolatry. It is crucial, though, that one do not think the alien thought intentionally. That is the meaning of "*ikvotecha* were not known," i.e., they are without intent.[122]

The Maggid identifies those to whom the principle applies, as opposed to all others. They are pious people immersed in Torah-study, continuously ascending from level to level with *deveikut* and *hitlahavut* to the point of their thoughts being attached to a level that transcends all worldly matters. They merit Divine assistance in purifying even their physical and material aspects. Alien thoughts occur to them in their prayers or studies (when they are immersed in, and attached to, holiness) in order that they may be sublimated to that holiness. Of these people he says: "You are not like the other people whose alien thoughts come to them from their own thought that is not purified from physical matters. You

---

121. See *Sifre, Shoftim,* par. 175; *Yevamot* 90b; and Maimonides, *Hilchot Yessodei Hatorah* 9:3.

122. *Or Torah,* sect. 231. Cf. *Maggid Devarav Leya'akov,* sect. 228, and *Or Torah,* sect. 277.

who walk in my statutes, when you are beset by an alien thought you can elevate it to holiness."[123]

The Maggid's disciples spell out these warnings in most explicit terms. R. Schneur Zalman of Liadi writes: "If there occur to [man] lustful imaginings or other alien thoughts at the time of worship, in [the study of] Torah or in devout prayer, he is not to take notice of them but immediately avert his mind from them. He should not be a fool and engage in the elevation of the traits of the alien thought, as is well known, for those things were meant only for *tzadikim* to whom alien thoughts do not occur of their own making but those of others. But he, to whom [an alien thought] occurs of his own making, i.e., from the aspect of evil in his heart ... how can he elevate it when he himself is bound [there], down below!"[124]

R. Meshulam Feivish of Zborez writes: "This should be your rule. Surely you understand this on your own, but the writings of that holy man, R. Dov Ber, of blessed memory, have become disclosed to various people, and there are but few who can compare themselves to him and act as he did, even minutely. They see there that he writes in a number of places.. that from the evil love that occurs in man he can attach himself to the love of the Creator.. and likewise with evil fear, base self-glorification, sense of triumph etc. This derivation can be applied only by one who is stripped of materialism. For if one is attached to materialism and desires, and willingly derives pleasure from them, then it is most certain that he knows

---

123. *Likkutim Yekarim*, sect. 118; *Or Torah*, sect. 123; cited (partially) in *Keter Shem Tov*, sect. 207.

124. *Tanya*, ch. 28 (p. 35a). R. Tzvi Elimelech of Dinov cites this passage repeatedly in his *Derech Pikudecha* (*Hakdamah* VII, par. 6-8; *Lo Ta'aseh* 35, 3:5; and *Lo Ta'aseh* 41, 3:4-5; ed. Lemberg 1921, pp. 13b-c, 86c, and 94df.). See also R. Menachem Mendel of Vitebsk, *Peri Ha'aretz*, *Vayigash*.

nothing of the love of the Creator, nor of the fear and glorification of [God] etc. ... Heaven forbid, he will fall into a deep pit if he will not watch himself very much. Only he who is divested of materialism and none the less it happens occasionally that an evil love or an evil fear awakens in his heart ... he is counseled to extract the precious from the vile... and will thereby be bestirred to a greater love of the Creator and fear of Him."[125]

R. David Shelomoh Eibeshitz[126] quotes at length this principle as taught by the Baal Shem Tov and reconciles it with the seemingly contradictory ruling of Maimonides[127] and the *Shulchan Aruch*[128] which ordains immediate dismissal of evil thoughts and directing the mind to words of Torah: "Both are true. Man must examine himself. If he guards himself very carefully not to blemish the aspects within his control, i.e., never to blemish by speech or act ... then evil thoughts will never occur to him.. The thought that will yet come to him [in spite of himself] occurs for the sake of correction, thus it is not to be repelled, as stated by the Baal Shem Tov, of blessed memory. But he who is not guarded in his spirit and soul, i.e., with his words and deeds, imaginings will occur to him on account of his own evil: they are altogether evil and will not be corrected. Heaven forbid for him to dwell on these thoughts even for a moment. He must push off and kill [that thought], as stated by Maimonides and the *Shulchan Aruch*."[129]

---

125. *Yosher Divrei Emet*, ch. 17 (p. 118b), cited (partially) in *Keter Shem Tov*, sect. 240. See there also the sequel (based on the sources cited above, note 120), and ch. 18.

126. Disciple of R. Wolf of Tsherni-Ostrow (a leading disciple of the Maggid) and R. Meshulam Feivish of Zborez, and author of *Levushei Serad* (a prominent commentary on *Shulchan Aruch*) and the classic *Arvei Nachal*.

127. *Hilchot Issurei Bi'ah* 21:19.

128. *Even Ha'ezer* 23:3.

129. *Arvei Nachal, Vayeira*, on Genesis 21:1-2 (ed. Warsaw, n.d., p. 39c).

B. The selfsame distinction applies also to the concept of "*Yeridah Tzorech Aliyah*—descent for the sake of an ascent." This concept relates to the principle of sublimating alien thoughts: "'Many waters cannot extinguish the love.' (Song 8:7) Alien thoughts are referred to as 'many waters,' the waves of the sea: 'those who go down to the sea' (Psalms 107:23), into the depths [of the sea], thus lowering themselves from their level in order that they may ascend, which is called a descent; but this descent is for the sake of an ascent, 'they do [their] work in many waters, they have seen the deeds of God...' (*ibid.*), for God is present even in those deeds."[130]

More often, however, this principle is cited in the more delicate context of the *tzadik's* "fall" to levels, situations or behavior that seems removed from, and inconsistent with, *deveikut* in general and his status in particular. He appears to engage in idle talk and inconsequential actions like the average person:

"The *tzadik* will sometimes fall from his level. This, however, is not a real 'fall,' as it is written, 'For a *tzadik* falls seven times and rises up again' (Proverbs 24:16): his very fall is but for the 'rising,' i.e., that [as he re-ascends] he will raise additional sparks along with himself. This is the meaning of 'he crouched and lay down like a lion' (Numbers 24:9), as it is said[131] that a lion goes down (crouches) only to seize prey [that he smells from afar]. So, too, the *tzadik* falls only for the sake of ascending, to raise sparks along with himself."[132]

"The *tzadik*, who is in a continuous state of *deveikut*, sometimes experiences a cessation of the *deveikut*. He should not be afraid [that this means] that he is removed from [God], be-

---

130. *Maggid Devarav Leya'akov*, sect. 10 and 235.
131. *Zohar* I:237b
132. *Maggid Devarav Leya'akov*, sect. 177; *Or Torah*, sect. 248, and *cf.* there also sect. 336.

cause this may possibly happen to him in order to attain a level
that is yet higher and excelling. The descent is for the sake of
an ascent, the being distanced is for the sake of coming
closer."[133]

This concept appears in our text as well.[134] It should be
quite obvious that it is filled with serious implications. The
Baal Shem Tov and the Maggid were fully conscious of these,
thus found it necessary to voice caution and qualifications:

"The ultimate intent in man being created with matter and
form is to refine the matter, so that matter is transformed into
form. This is the meaning of 'That man do [the *mitzvot*] and
live by them' (Leviticus 18:5), as Nachmanides comments (*ad
loc.*) that this relates to various levels and aspects. One aspect is
that after ascending on high one descends again in order to
elevate the lower levels. Every descent, however, requires caution to re-ascend, lest he remain there, Heaven forbid, as the
Baal Shem Tov said that there are many who remained [be-
low]."[135]

There is a clear emphasis in practically all references to this
principle that it applies only to the *tzadik,* the spiritually accomplished person who is firmly fastened to Above to assure
that he will ascend again after the "fall."[136]

---

133. *Or Torah*, sect. 427.

134. See sect. 64 and 96.

135. *Toldot Ya'akov Yossef, Vayeira:*I (p. 59a-b), cited (in amended wording) in
Keter Shem Tov, sect. 90 and 396.

136. Note carefully *Likkutim Yekarim*, sect. 113, and *Or Torah*, sect. 488, illus-
trating the point with a parable that appears in *Zohar* I:112b: "When
Abraham descended to Egypt, and when he went to the land of the Philis-
tines, he [first] attached himself to the faith. [This is comparable] to a
person who wants to descend into a deep pit, but is afraid that he will be
unable to ascend from the pit. What did he do? He tied a rope above the
pit, saying: 'As I made this bond, from now on I can enter [the pit].' So,
too, with Abraham: when he wanted to go down to Egypt, prior to de-

Moreover, the consistent expression of "when he falls," or "sometimes falls," indicates passivity. In other words, as in the case of alien thoughts that are to be elevated, it is not an intentional fall or descent, but just happens by Divine Providence. The very same qualifications relating to the sublimation of alien thoughts apply equally to the general principle of *yeridah tzorech aliyah*.

The Maggid spells this out in sharp and unequivocal terms:

"In all matters one is to serve God continuously [in a mode of] *avodat gevohah* ('for the sake of Above;' exclusively for the sake of God without any ulterior motives). One is not to be, Heaven forbid, like those licentious ones who say that man must make himself descend to the lowest level and then ascend from there, i.e., *yeridah tzorech aliyah*. This must not happen [among the people of] Israel. A number of people left the faith on account of such![137]

"It follows that man must be continuously attached unto [God], blessed be His Name. If he should fall from his level, Heaven forbid, he must quickly restore himself to the higher level.

"These matters are too lengthy to be explained. But it is beyond human ability, and if he were to do so he will fall and not rise. Thus it is explained in the *Zohar* (I:117a), with reference to "'I shall go through Egypt' (Exodus 12:12)—i.e., I [God Himself], and not an angel, 'and I will smite ...' (*ibid.*)—i.e., I, and not a *seraph.*"[138]: Egypt was a place of impurity to the

---

scending there, he first tied the bond of the faith to be strengthened by it, and then he descended there." *Cf.* also the similar passage in *Zohar* I:81b, cited and explained in our context in *Toldot Ya'akov Yossef, Nasso:*XVII, and *Degel Machaneh Ephrayim*, beg. of *Shemot*.

137. *Cf.* the Baal Shem Tov's warning, cited above (re note 133).

138. *Mechilta* on Exodus 12:12 and 12:29; cited in the *Haggadah for Pesach*.

point that that if an angel had gone there he would have [become and] remained defiled, Heaven forbid. The light of the Holy One, blessed is He, however, penetrates everything, and nothing can interpose before Him. This, however, is not in the power of man.

"Thus 'You shall be only above' (Deuteronomy 28:23), i.e., to serve God on the level of 'above' (the high level), 'and you shall not be below' (ibid.), i.e., on the level of 'below'— i.e., on the lower level, as stated ..."[139]

III
TARGET OF OPPOSITION TO CHASSIDISM

Tzava'at Harivash is one of the early publications of Chassidism, but was printed later than the works of the Maggid and R. Ya'akov Yossef of Polnoy. Thus one cannot ascribe to it special significance, because most of its teachings appeared already in those earlier books. Nonetheless, it became a primary target in the attacks by the opponents to Chassidism. Their criticisms against Chassidic teachings refer specifically to *Tzava'at Harivash* and they had public burnings of the book.[140] Two reasons may account for singling out this work:

1) *Tzava'at Harivash* is a very small book. It may even be called a pamphlet. The first editions consisted of 48 small pages (including the title-page), approximately 3 by 5 inches. Thus it must have been quite inexpensive, allowing for wide distribution. Moreover, the smallness of the book as a whole, and the brevity of its individual teachings, make it a very read-

---

139. *Likkutei Amarim*-Vitebsk, p. 25bf.; *Likkutei Amarim*—MS. of R. Shmelka of Nikolsburg I:14 (facsimile of this passage appears in *Torat Hamaggid Mimezhirech*, p. [9]).

140. See M. Wilensky, *Chassidim UMitnagdim* (a study of the controversy between them in the years 1772-1815), Jerusalem 1970, vol. I, pp. 182, 201, 202, 252, 267 and 289.

able text for friend and foe alike, unlike the earlier texts that were much bulkier and much more intricate. Little wonder, then, that it gained great popularity: there were at least seven editions between 1792 and 1797![141] This must surely have concerned the *Mitnagdim* (adversaries to Chassidism) and aroused their ire.

2) *Tzava'at Harivash* is a specialized anthology of Chassidic teachings. It consists of pericopes that present explicit guidance, "instructions and rules of proper conduct," taught by the Baal Shem Tov and the Maggid, the founders and leaders of the Chassidic movement and Chassidic philosophy. It is a manual for the religious life and observance of the chassid. It addresses the masses no less than the scholars. Our text can then be seen as an easily identifiable manifesto of Chassidism. Thus it became the logical choice to be a prime target for those who opposed Chassidism.

The adversaries' accusations against the teachings in *Tzava'at Harivash* are as follows:[142]

(a) Sect. 41 is a denigration of Torah and Torah-study.[143] (b) The segment of sect. 44-46 furthers illicit frivolity.[144] More specifically, sect. 44 errs in dismissing depression and in calling thoughts leading to depression "evil";[145] sect. 45 (as well as

---

141. See the bibliographical list appended to my Hebrew edition of *Tzava'at Harivash*.

142. The synopsis following is culled from the writings of the adversaries that were published in M. Wilensky, *Chassidim Umitnagdim*, and from the documents recently discovered in the archives of the prosecutor-general in S. Petersburg (see below, note 161) and published in *Kerem Chabad* IV:1, Kfar Chabad 1992 (henceforward abbreviated as KC).

143. *Sefer Viku'ach*, pp. 300 and 307f.

144. *Ibid.*, p. 306; *Zemir Aritzim*, p. 212. See also *Shever Poshim*, p. 135; and *cf. Zemir Aritzim Vechorbot Tzurim*, p. 38.

145. Depositions of Avigdor Chaimovitch (henceforward: Avigdor), p. 249ff. Note also *Zemir Aritzim*, p. 212: "In the books of R. Israel Baal Shem is

sect. 107) errs in dismissing weeping in prayer;[146] and sect. 46 suggests anti-nomianism.[147] (c) Sect. 64 (as well as sect. 96), dealing with *yeridah tzorech aliyah*, suggests anti-nomianism.[148] (d) Sect. 68 is crude imagery leading to licentiousness.[149] (e) Sect. 74 is a denigration of Torah-study and the normative religious lifestyle.[150] (f) Sect. 87: i. To say that one need not fear anything but God is absurd and contradicts Scripture. ii. To say that a Divine life-force is vested in all beings, including animals, is blasphemy. iii. To say that everything happening to man is by Divine Providence is to justify all wrongdoing and to exempt all wrong-doers from punishment.[151] (g) Sect. 108: to say that in prayer one becomes unified with God is unfounded "worthless illusions."[152] (h) Sect. 109 furthers licentiousness and anti-nomianism by suggesting the indulgence of all desires.[153] (i) Sect. 120 is blasphemous for stating that the *Shechinah* is vested in all human beings.[154] (j) Sect. 127 errs i. in relating the Divine glory to creatures; ii. in stating that there is a Divine emanation in all beings; iii. in stating that one is to love and fear God alone; and iv. to identify speech

---

written that it is forbidden to bring depression upon oneself. In truth, if that had been the sole content of his books, [they] would already deserve to be cast unto fire to be condemned to burning."

146. *Sefer Viku'ach*, p. 306; Avigdor, p. 249*ff.*, and in KC, p. 82.

147. *Sefer Viku'ach*, pp. 306 and 309. Cf. *Zemir Aritzim Vechorbot Tzurim*, p. 38.

148. *Sefer Viku'ach*, pp. 298 and 312.

149. *Shever Poshim*, pp. 102f. and 108; *Zemir Aritzim*, p. 214. It is noteworthy that, aside of the fact that erotic metaphors are common to all Kabbalistic writings, some of the very same terms that the adversaries objected to are used by the Gaon of Vilna in his commentaries on the *Zohar*! See KC, p. 160*f.*

150. *Sefer Viku'ach*, p. 310*f.*

151. Avigdor, p. 273; and in KC, p. 83.

152. *Ibid.*, pp. 248 and 274; and in KC, p. 83.

153. *Ibid.*, pp. 248f. and 273; and in KC, p. 83.

154. *Zemir Aritzim*, p. 312.

with the vital force of God inherent in man is a blasphemous attribution of man's lies and evil speech to God.[155] (k) Sect. 137: i. To say that one must always be "merry and joyous" is wrong, because rejoicing is restricted to the celebration of the festivals in the Holy Temple, and is not allowed even in prayer. This statement thus proves that "they are of the cult of Shabbatai Tzvi," because it assumes that the Messiah has come already. ii. To believe that "the kindness of God dwells upon man and embraces him" contradicts Scripture which relates that Jacob was afraid in spite of the Divine promise to be with him everywhere (Genesis 28:15). Thus "one cannot establish this kind of trust in God." iii. To say that "man sees God and God sees man" is a blasphemous ascription of corporeality to God.[156]

Not surprisingly, there is an implicit attack on the concept of sublimation of alien thoughts,[157] though without a specific reference.[158] The over-all criticism by the *Mitnagdim* of the Chassidic adoption of the Lurianic-Sefardi liturgy[159] also touches upon *Tzava'at Harivash*, for sect. 143 explains a notable difference between that text and the Ashkenazy one.

Eight of the references cited above appear in the slanderous accusations before the Czarist regime by Avigdor Chaimovitch of Pinsk against R. Schneur Zalman of Liadi. Avigdor submitted two depositions: the first was addressed to the authorities, and the second one was to be given by them to R. Schneur Zalman for his response. There are notable differences between the two: Avigdor is much more careful with the

---

155. Avigdor, pp. 246*ff.* and 274; and in KC, p. 83.
156. Ibid., pp. 244*f.* and 246; and in KC, p. 82.
157. *Shever Poshim*, p. 148*f.*; *Sefer Viku'ach*, p. 308.
158. See above, *s.v.* Sublimation of Alien Thoughts.
159. See also Y. Mundshein, "*Kinat HaMitnagdim Leminhagei Ashkenaz,*" KC, p. 151*ff.*

criticisms in the second deposition, omitting many of his alleged refutations. He must have realized that they were blatantly absurd, thus easily dismissed. Even so, there is a consistent thread of misquotation and distortion running through both.[160] R. Schneur Zalman exposes these distortions, and offers clear and convincing explanations which vindicated *Tzava'at Harivash* and the Chassidic philosophy, and brought about his acquittal and liberation from imprisonment.[161]

The criticism of sect. 120 was again submitted to R. Schneur Zalman in a private (and apparently friendly and respectful) communication from *Mitnagdim*. His elaborate response, analyzing the relevant principles in great detail, implicitly answers also most of the criticisms against sect. 87 and 127. It overlaps in many respects with his lengthy response on sect. 87 in the court-case.[162]

---

160. This is a common feature in many of the early writings of the *Mitnagdim*; see Y. Mundshein, "*Siluf Divrei Chassidut,*" *ibid.,* p. 158*ff. Sefer Viku'ach* is a notable exception to this.

161. Avigdor's second deposition has 19 accusations against Chassidism and R. Schneur Zalman. All but the first two were known and published (Wilensky, vol. I, p. 273*ff.*). Of R. Schneur Zalman's responses only the last two were known and published (*ibid.,* p. 277). Recent research discovered the files of this case in the archives of the prosecutor-general in Petersburg. These include these last two answers in the original Hebrew handwriting of R. Schneur Zalman and signed by him. as well as the Russian translation of all his answers. They include also Avigdor's original Hebrew deposition (the second one), except for the first two charges, and a Russian translation of all. All this has now been published in *Kerem Chabad* IV:1, in Hebrew translation where necessary, including photostats of the originals. R. Schneur Zalman's submissions appear now also in *Igrot Kodesh—Admur Hazaken,* vol. II, pp. 39-62 and 140.

162. *Tanya, Igeret Hakodesh,* sect. 25 (pp. 138a-142a). *Cf.* also R. Schneur Zalman's letter to the Chassidim in Vilna, written in 1797, *Igrot Kodesh— Admur Hazaken,* vol. I, p. 88 (also in Wilensky, vol. I, p. 200).

TZAVA'AT HARIVASH

THE TESTAMENT
OF
RABBI ISRAEL
BAAL SHEM TOV

1

Testament[1] *of R. Israel Baal Shem, peace be upon him —*

Be complete in the worship [of God], blessed be He, [that it be] a "complete service."[2]

It is essential not to forget the matters [of Torah and *Mitzvot*].[3]

It is essential to study *mussar*[4] every day, whether much or little.

Strive continuously to cleave to good traits and upright practices.

Do not allow a single day to pass without performing a *mitzvah*, whether it be a "minor" or "major" *mitzvah*.[5] This is

---

1. This is not the Baal Shem Tov's testament in the sense of "last will." He did not leave a "last will" in writing or in words. *Tzava'ah* here means "instruction," i.e., instructions and guidelines taught by the Baal Shem Tov for the ideal religious conduct.

2. *Avodah tamah* is a Talmudic expression (*Yoma* 24a) denoting a form of service that is complete in itself without any further action required for its completion.

3. The sentence is not very clear. The wording is reminiscent of the Biblical phrase "[But take heed and watch yourself greatly lest] you forget the matters [that your eyes saw...]" (Deuteronomy 4:9-10), and perhaps alludes to it. It does not appear at all in *Keter Shem Tov* (p. 1b). In *Likkutim Yekarim* (no. 198) it is combined with the next sentence, reading: "It is essential not to forget to study *mussar* every day..." Our rendition, with the bracketed words, follows the interpretation in *Be'urim Betzava'at Harivash*, no. 2.

4. Works of moral guidance and inspiration. This would refer to texts like R. Bachya Ibn Pakuda's *Chovot Halevovot*, R. Eliahu de Vidas' *Reishit Chochmah*, R. Isaiah Horowitz's *Shenei Luchot Haberit*, and so forth, and no less so the pervasive *mussar* found in the *Zohar*. On the importance of studying *mussar*, see also below, sect. 117.

5. The emphasis is on *daily* acts. Every single day is an important entity on its own. Thus it requires something concrete to show for itself, a light or illumination of its own that is effected by the performance of a *mitzvah*. To perform many *mitzvot* on one day cannot make up for the lost opportunity

indicated in "Be *zahir* (careful; scrupulous) with a 'minor' *mitzvah* as with a 'major' one" (*Avot* 2:1). For [the word] *zahir* is an expression of "They that are wise *yaz'hiru* (shall shine)..." (Daniel 12:3). This implies that the soul will shine and glow from a "minor" *mitzvah* even as it does from a "major" one, for "The Merciful seeks the heart" (*Zohar* II:162b; *Sanhedrin* 106b).[6]

---

of another day. *Cf. Zohar* I:129a and 224a on the significance of each individual day.

6. "The Merciful seeks the heart, i.e., that man's heart should seek the Merciful." (*Likkutim Yekarim*, no. 106) To the seeker of God there is no difference between "major" and "minor" *mitzvot*: both are commands of God and effect refinement and illumination of the soul. *Cf.* below, sect. 122.

Note: this paragraph has an explanatory sequel below, sect. 17[a]; see there.

2-3

"*Shiviti*—I have set God before me at all times." (Psalms 16:8)

Shiviti is an expression of *hishtavut* (equanimity):[1] no matter what happens, whether people praise or shame you, and so, too, with anything else, it is all the same to you. This applies likewise to any food: it is all the same to you whether you eat delicacies or other things. For [with this perspective] the *yetzer hara* is entirely removed from you.

Whatever may happen, say that "it comes from [God], blessed be He, and if it is proper in His eyes..."[2] Your motives

---

1. *Shiviti* is related to the root-word *shaveh*, equal. The notion of equanimity is a fundamental principle in the pursuit of authentic religiosity and piety. R. Bachya ibn Pakuda (*Chovot Halevovot, Sha'ar Yichud Hama'aseh*, ch. 5) calls it the "ultimate of the most precious levels among the rungs of the pious." See also below, sect. 6, 10, 84, 91, 93 and 127.

2. Equanimity follows logically from a profound sense of *hashgachah peratit*, the belief that every detail is controlled by Divine Providence. Our proof-text

are altogether for the sake of Heaven, and as for yourself nothing makes any difference.

This [sense of equanimity] is a very high level.

Also, serve God with all your might, because everything is "required [for Above]."[3] God wishes to be served in all possible ways. This means the following:

Sometimes one may walk and talk to others and is then unable to study [Torah]. Nonetheless, you must attach yourself to God and effect *yichudim* (unifications).[4] So also when on the road, thus unable to pray and study as usual, you must serve [God] in other ways.

Do not be disturbed by this. For God wishes to be served in all possible ways, sometimes in one manner and sometimes in another. That is why it happened that you had to go on a journey or talk to people, i.e., in order that you serve Him in that alternate way.

---

thus reads: "*Shiviti*—everything is equal to me [*because* I realize that] God is before me at all times." See below, sect. 4.

3. *Tzorech gevoha*, lit. "for the need of Above." This is the mystical term indicating that everything in creation is to be for the Divine intent, i.e., for the realization of the ultimate perfection of the spiritual reality underlying physical reality: "God has made everything for His own purpose." (Proverbs 16:4) *Cf.* below, sect. 11 and 73.

4. *Yichudim* (unifications) is the Kabbalistic concept of effecting harmony in the totality of creation by "connecting" (unifying) things to their spiritual roots. See below, sect. 22, 75, 94 and 123.

4

An important rule: "Commit your deeds to God, and your thoughts shall be established." (Proverbs 16:3) That is, you must realize that whatever happens is from [God], blessed be He.[1]

---

1. The realization of *hashgachah peratit*; see above, sect. 2, note 2.

See to it that you request from God always to visit upon you that which God knows to be for your benefit, as opposed to that which appears to be so to the human mind.[2] For it is quite possible that what is good in your own eyes is really bad for you. Thus commit unto God everything, all your concerns and needs.

---

2.   *Cf.* above, sect. 2, and below, sect. 84.

5-6

Attach your thought to Above.[1] Do not eat or drink excessively, but only to the extent of maintaining your health.[2] Never look intently at mundane matters, nor pay any attention to them, so that you may be separated from the physical. Intent viewing of the mundane brings crudity upon oneself. Our sages, of blessed memory, thus said that "sight leads to remembering and to desire;"[3] and it is written of the Tree of Knowledge that it is "desirable to the sight and good for eating" (Genesis 2:9), i.e., the sight of it made it desirable.

Think that you belong to the Supernal World and all the people dwelling in this world should not be important to you.

---

1.   I.e., the focus of your thought should always be on the supernal spirituality, as opposed to the mundane. Thus you yourself, too, will be attached to spirituality (see below, sect. 69). *Cf.* below, sect. 8 and 24.

2.   See Maimonides, *Hilchot De'ot* 3:2 and ch. 4.

3.   Man is affected by what he sees, positively or negatively. To view something good or holy has positive effects. For example, to gaze at the *tzitzit* (ritual fringes on certain garments, ordained in Numbers 15:38ff.) will lead to observance of *mitzvot*, as it is written "you will *see* it and *remember* all the commandments of God and *do* them" (*ibid.* verse 39). In turn, to gaze at the physical and mundane will arouse desires related to it and, therefore, lead to wrongful actions in their pursuit: "The eyes see and the heart covets, and the body commits the sin." (Commentary of Rashi on Numbers 15:39) See also below, sect. 121, and *cf.* sect. 50 and 90.

For the whole of this world is but like a granule in relation to the Supernal World. Be indifferent to others loving you or hating you, for their love or hatred means nothing. Likewise, do not pay any attention to the desires of your filthy body which is a "leprous thing from the skin of the snake."[4]

---

4. The phrase is from *Tikunei Zohar* 21:48b. The physical body seeks physical pleasure that defiles and leads astray, even as the original serpent enticed Adam and Eve. This does not mean, however, that the body is evil *per se*. It is the outer garment to the soul, allowing the soul to function in this world with the performance of *mitzvot*. Thus it is not equivalent to the serpent but only to the "skin of the serpent," i.e., its external aspect. As such it is an admixture of good and evil, allowing man's freedom of choice to do good or evil (see *ibid.* 67:98a)

7-8

The *Zohar* (III:195a) states that one's will is to be like that of a pauper.[1] Thus consider yourself like a pauper and always speak with soft and beseeching words like a pauper.

Your thought should always be secluded with the *Shechinah*,[2] thinking only of your continuous love for Her that She may be attached to you. Say constantly in your mind: "When will I merit that the light of the *Shechinah* abide with me?"[3]

---

1. "Which is the most excellent of all [prayers]? It is the prayer of the poor.. it takes precedence to all prayers of the world.. because he is broken-hearted, and it is written, 'God is near to the broken-hearted' (Psalms 34:19).. Thus, when praying, a person should make himself poor.. When a person.. will always make his will as that of a pauper, his prayer ascends.. and will be received favorably before the Holy King."
2. See above, sect. 5-6, note 1.—The term *Shechinah* signifies the Divine immanence and presence throughout the world, the Divine "spark" and life-force (vitality) in all creatures. (*Shechinah* is always referred to in feminine gender.)
3. As man attaches himself to God through *mitzvot* and communion, the light of the *Shechinah* becomes ever more manifest to him.

9

When beset by mundane desires, remove them from your mind. Scorn the desire to the point of it becoming hated and despised by you.[1] Incite the *yetzer tov* against the *yetzer hara* and your desire, and thus you will subdue them.[2]

Do not be depressed at all from not having mundane desires. On the contrary, rejoice exceedingly for meriting to subdue your passion for the sake of the Creator's glory, may He be blessed. Our sages said of this, "rejoicing in the suffering" (*Shabbat* 88b).

When you are not drawn after your desire, even in thought, and scorn it, you subdue the *kelipot*[3] very much, as it is said in the *Zohar* (I:100b): "'A pure heart' (Psalms 24:4) is the one that will not let his will and heart be drawn after the *sitra achara*."[4]

---

1. See above, sect. 5-6.
2. See *Berachot* 5a: "Man should always incite the *yetzer tov* (good impulse in man) against the *yetzer hara* (evil impulse in man) [i.e., to wage battle against the *yetzer hara*; Rashi], as it is written 'Tremble (incite) and sin not (*or*: and you will not sin)' (Psalms 4:5)." To do so, helps subdue the personal *yetzer hara* and the power of evil (that is concentrated in worldly pleasures) in general, as explained below.

   Note the term "subdues." It accords with the Baal Shem Tov's interpretation of "Who is strong? He who conquers (subdues) his [evil] impulse" (*Avot* 4:1): the *yetzer hara* is not to be destroyed but conquered, i.e., to harness its energy for good, to utilize it for matters of holiness. (*Cf. Shenei Luchot Haberit*, Bet David (cur. ed. p. 16b; also *ibid.* p. 36b.)
3. "*Kelipah* (pl. *kelipot*)—husk(s); shell(s)" (analogous to the crude husk that encompasses the edible fruit) is the mystical term for the realm or forces of evil and impurity.
4. "*Sitra achara*—the other side," i.e., the "side of evil and impurity," as opposed to the "side of holiness." Sinful thoughts and acts vitalize and strengthen the *sitra achara* (see below, sect. 87 and 90; and *cf.* sect. 43, note 8). In turn, overcoming and subduing such thoughts and temptations subdues and weakens the *kelipot* (see below, sect. 79).

10

Equanimity is an important principle.[1] This means that it should be all the same to you whether you are regarded as devoid of knowledge or learned in the whole Torah. This [perspective] is brought about by constant *deveikut* (attachment) unto the Creator.[2] Preoccupation with this *deveikut*, being constantly busy with attaching yourself on high to [God], blessed is He, will not leave any spare time to think of those [other] matters.[3]

1. See above, sect. 2.
2. *Deveikut*—attachment, cleaving, unto God. In mystical writings *deveikut* signifies intimate communion with God. It is a dominant theme in Chassidic teachings in general, and in our text in particular.
3. See below, sect. 52.

11

Whatever you do, have in mind to give gratification to your Creator, blessed be He, and do not think—even a little—of your own needs.[1] Even the expectation of personal delight from your service [of God] is [an ulterior motive] for one's own concerns.[2]

1. I.e., the concept of "service for the sake of Above" (see sect. 2-3). This is the principle of "Acknowledge Him in all your ways" (Proverbs 3:6; see below, sect. 94), and "Let all your deeds be for the sake of Heaven" (*Avot* 2:12), as explained in *Shulchan Aruch, Orach Chayim*:231.
2. True service of God implies total disregard of self, to the point of *bitul hayesh*, self-negation (see below, sect. 52-53). This excludes the expectation of any sort of reward (material or spiritual), the pursuit of spiritual attainments (*cf.* below, sect. 47), let alone a sense of self-satisfaction. All these are *peniyot* (sing. *peniyah*), ulterior motives of ego-centricity that must be shunned (see below, sect. 15, 42, 55, 77 and 92).

12

Do not think that by worshipping with *deveikut*[1] you are greater than another. You are like any other creature, created for the sake of His worship, blessed be He. God gave a mind to the other just as He gave a mind to you.

What makes you superior to a worm? The worm serves the Creator with all its mind and strength![2] Man, too, is a worm and maggot, as it is written "I am a worm and no man." (Psalms 22:7) If God had not given you intelligence you would not be able to worship Him but like a worm. Thus you are no better than a worm, and certainly [no better] than [other] people.

Bear in mind that you, the worm and all other small creatures are considered as equals in the world. For all were created and have but the ability given to them by the blessed Creator.[3]

Always keep this matter in mind.

---

1. See above, sect. 11, note 2.
2. All created things praise and worship God, each in its own way, as described in the *Midrash Perek Shirah*. See there especially the preamble (cited in *Yalkut Shimoni* on Psalms 150) how King David was rebuked by a frog who demonstrated that its service of God excels that of King David.
3. As each creature serves God according to its own abilities, all are proportionally equal. That man can and will do more than others, therefore, is no reason for self-satisfaction or arrogance: he can do so only by virtue of the special abilities given to him by God. *Cf.* below, sect. 48.

13-14

When tempted to commit a sin, [Heaven forbid,] recite the [Biblical] verses pertaining to that sin. [Recite them] with their intonations and punctuation, with fear and love [of God], and [the temptation] will leave you.[1]

When tempted by an evil trait, Heaven forbid, recite with all might, with fear and love [of God], [the names of] the six nations—the Canaanite etc.[2] Thus it will depart from you.

---

1. Torah, in general, is the antidote to the *yetzer hara*, the impulse and temptation to sin (see below, beginning of sect. 138). Reciting the specific verses that relate to the subject of the sinful temptation, in the manner prescribed here, will negate the temptation. (If the sin has already been committed it will correct this in conjunction with *teshuvah*; see *Maggid Devarav Leya'akov*, sect. 223).

2. All aspects in the realm of holiness and purity have corresponding counterparts in the realm of evil and impurity (see below, sect. 139, note 3). Thus just as there are the attributes (*Sefirot*) of holiness, so there are the attributes of impurity (*Zohar* III:41b and 70a). In terms of man, therefore, there are the "good" traits of *chessed* and *gevurah* (manifested in *love* and *fear* of God, for example; pursuit of the good, and self-negation or avoidance of that which is forbidden). Their corresponding "evil" traits would be, e.g., love of, and attraction to, the mundane or the forbidden; to be afraid of that which one should not fear, or negation of another human as expressed in anger and hatred, and so forth. (*Cf.* below, sect. 87.)

    Seven nations inhabited the Land of Israel before the Jewish people came there after the exodus. As they were morally corrupt, they were to be expelled from there (Deuteronomy 7:1*ff.* and 20:16*ff.*). In Kabbalistic terminology they correspond to the seven *midot* (emotive attributes of the ten *Sefirot*—*chessed, gevurah, tiferet, netzach, hod, yessod* and *malchut*) of *sitra achara* (as opposed to the *midot* of the realm of holiness); see below, sect. 87, and *cf. Maggid Devarav Leya'akov*, sect. 110 and 147. In our context, temptation of any sinful trait or emotion in man is rooted in them. Thus reciting their names "with fear and love of God" leads to an awareness that sinful desires derive from evil, must be conquered and expelled, and this will remove the temptation.

    Our text refers to "six nations." In the Torah, too, we find that mostly only six are named, omitting the Girgashite. According to tradition, the Girgashite fled the land before the Israelites entered and, therefore, there was no need to expel them. In our context, the Girgashite, signifying the attribute of *malchut* (kingship; sovereignty) of the realm of impurity, is of no concern: *malchut*, the last of the seven attributes, is merely like a "filter" for

Connect that trait unto the Holy One, blessed be He. For example, if tempted by sinful love, Heaven forbid, channel all your love to God alone and concentrate all your efforts in that direction. When [tempted] by anger, which is an expression of sinful "fear" and derives from the attribute of *gevurah*, overpower your *yetzer [hara]* and transform that trait into a chariot for God.[3]

When you hear someone preach with fear and love [of God], attach yourself strongly to his words to become united with the preacher. His words will then become thoughts in your mind and [the sinful thought] will leave you.[4]

---

the compound of the first six; thus as the earlier six are "corrected," the seventh is dispelled of itself.

3. Sinful thoughts or desires are overcome in one of two ways: (i) Driving them away by diversion of thought, i.e., disregarding them altogether and filling your mind with positive thoughts. (ii) Elevation or sublimation of the evil thought or desire to goodness. This is a frequent theme in early Chassidic teachings of which this paragraph is a typical example (and see also below, sect. 22, 87, 90, 101, 120 and 127).

Chassidic texts, from the earliest onwards, caution emphatically that the second method is a hazardous technique that should be employed only by those who have reached spiritual perfection. Others may be led yet further astray by it, thus must not even attempt it.

4. This last paragraph is another way to rid yourself of sinful thoughts: concentrating on, and filling your mind with, positive thoughts of holiness will of itself dispel the negative thoughts.

15

First and foremost be careful that every motion in the Divine service be without ulterior motives, Heaven forbid.[1] This requires profound wisdom "exceedingly deep, who can find it out?" (Ecclesiastes 7:24) There is then no alternative but to

---

1. See above, sect. 11, especially note 2. Ulterior motives may be the first step of spiritual decline.

retain constant awareness of this principle. Do not divert your mind from it, even for a moment, for it is a matter that is flawed by distraction.

Secondly, you must also be scrupulous with [ritual] immersion, and to concentrate in the *mikveh* on the appropriate *kavanot* (devotions) for *mikveh*.[2]

For the "three-fold cord that is not broken quickly" (Ecclesiastes 4:12): remove yourself from depression and let your heart rejoice in God.[3]

---

2. Immersion in a *mikveh* (ritual pool or equivalent) is mandated by the Torah for removal of impurity. It serves also for those who are pure to attain higher levels of spiritual purity required by Torah-law. Mystics, therefore, encourage emphatically frequent immersions in context of the Divine service. It is common practice among Chassidim to immerse daily (except when precluded to do so by law, as on *Yom Kippur*) before the morning-prayers, aside of the additional immersions before the onset of every *Shabbat* or festival. They did and do so even in the most difficult conditions, such as in rivers or lakes in the winter. Kabbalistic and Chassidic texts offer a number of special *kavanot* for the immersions.

   The Baal Shem Tov said (*Keter Shem Tov*, Addenda, sect. 164) that proper immersion is effective even without any *kavanah* (cf. *Chulin* 31a, and *Shulchan Aruch*, Yoreh De'ah 198:48 and 201:5). In Halachah, however, this applies only to the basic purification for *chulin* (ordinary, unconsecrated matters), but not for something that is consecrated. Immersion for greater purification for matters of Torah, prayer and sacred matters, therefore, ought to have at least the proper intent towards that end (e.g., for the sake of purity or *teshuvah*). See at length *Sefer Baal Shem Tov*, Yitro, note 19.

   A statement nearly identical to the present one appears as a sequel in the parallel-version of sect. 1 above (and sect. 17-19 below) in *Likkutim Yekarim*, sect. 198: "One is to immerse as much as possible, especially when required to do so, and to meditate in the *mikveh* on the appropriate meditations." Note there also, sect. 178 (which appears also in the Maggid's *Or Torah*, sect. 205-d), that the Baal Shem Tov "merited all his illumination and levels by virtue of his frequent immersions. Continuous use of the *mikveh* is much better than fasting..."

3. This is another fundamental principle of Chassidism, often repeated at length in this text (see below, sect. 44-46, 56, 107, 110 and end of 137).

16

It is necessary to make it known that one should regularly [rise] at midnight.[1]

At the very least be scrupulous to recite the [morning]-prayer before sunrise, both in summer and winter. That is, most of the prayer, up to the reading of the *Shema*, should be said before sunrise.[2] The difference between before sunrise and after sunrise is as great as the distance from east to west; for prior [to sunrise] one can still negate [all judgments].[3] This is indicated in [the verse], "[The sun is] like a groom coming forth from his bridal chamber, rejoicing like a war-

---

1. The night is a propitious time for Torah-study (see *Chagigah* 12b; *Tamid* 32b; *et passim*). This applies especially to midnight which is an especially auspicious time of Divine grace and favor (*Yevamot* 72a). Thus "Bless God, all you *servants of God who stand in the House of God in the nights*" (Psalms 134:1); these ("who stand.. in the nights") are the true servants of God, worthy to bless Him (see *Menachot* 110a, and *Zohar* I:136a). King David, therefore, never allowed a midnight to pass asleep, as he said (Psalms 119:62) "At midnight I arise to give thanks.." (*Berachot* 3b)

   With the destruction of the *Bet Hamikdash* (the Holy Temple in Jerusalem), midnight became the time that God Himself mourns that catastrophe and the subsequent exile of Israel (*Berachot, ibid.*). Thus it became a special time for Israel, too, to mourn and lament its exile and to pray for the redemption (*Rosh* on *Berachot, ad loc.; Shulchan Aruch, Orach Chayim,* sect. 1). This is known as *tikun chatzot,* the midnight vigil with a special order of prayers followed by the study of Torah in general, and selected passages from Talmud and *Zohar* in particular.

   The mystics are very emphatic on the practice of study and prayer at night, and it is a recurring theme in our text as well (see below, sect. 26-28 and 83).

2. This is the ideal time for the morning-prayer (*Berachot* 29b), and "*vatikin*— those who are strong (in piety, i.e., those who love the performance of the commandments) would complete (the reading of the *Shema*) with sunrise" (*ibid.* 9b).

3. That part of the day is an especially auspicious time, as stated in *Mechilta* and *Zohar*.

rior.. and nothing is hidden from *chamato* (its heat)" (Psalms 19:6-7); do not read *chamota* (its heat) but *cheimato* (his wrath). This means that once the sun has already risen over the earth there is no more hiding from the judgments which come from the angels of wrath. Thus do not regard this matter lightly, for it is of great import. The Baal Shem, may his memory be for blessing, was very particular with this, to the point that when he did not have a quorum he would pray on his own.

17-19

a. Do not allow a single day to pass without performing a *mitzvah*, whether it be a "minor" or "major" *mitzvah*, as our sages said, "Be *zahir* (careful; scrupulous) with a 'minor' *mitzvah* [as with a 'major' one]" (*Avot* 2:1): the word *zahir* is an idiom of "They that are wise *yaz'hiru* (shall shine)." (Daniel 12:3). This means that the soul will shine and glow from a "minor" *mitzvah* even as it does from a "major" one, for "The Merciful requires the heart" (*Zohar* II:162b; *Sanhedrin* 106b).[1] This is a very significant matter, for then you know that you achieved something that day: you created an angel,[2] and "if there be for him an angel, an intercessor..." (Job 33:23)[3]

---

1. Up to here is a repetition of the third paragraph in sect. 1; see there notes 5-6.

2. "When anyone performs good deeds, i.e., the commandments, each *mitzvah* he did ascends on high, stands before the Holy One, blessed is He, and says: 'I am from so-and-so who did me.' The Holy One, blessed is He, then provides that person with an angel that will help him.. Likewise, the Holy One, blessed is He, provides him with an angel for every word of Torah that he listens to." (*Zohar Chadash*, Acharei:47a)

   See also *Avot* 4:11: "He who does even a single *mitzvah* gains himself an advocate; and he who commits a single sin acquires an accuser."

3. "Even if 999 [accusers] argue for his guilt, and one [advocate] argues in his favor, he is saved, as it is said, 'If there be with him an angel, an intercessor, one among a thousand . . . He is gracious to him.'" (*Shabbat* 32a)

This is indicated [in the verse] "*shomer mitzvah* (he who guards the *mitzvah* will know no evil" (Ecclesiastes 8:5). That is, when you undertake the instruction stated, you must stand on guard from morning to evening for the opportunity to perform a *mitzvah* that may come your way. This is the implication of the word *shomer*, as in "his father *shamar* (guarded; awaited and looked forward to) the matter" (Genesis 37:11). It is the remedy [to attain] "he will know no evil," i.e., precluding nocturnal emissions which are referred to as "evil."[4]

[This general principle] is indicated [in the verse], "The kindness of God is *kol hayom* ("all day long"; or: "every day") (Psalms 52:3); that is, one needs perform kindness with God, blessed is He,[5] every single day.

b. Guard the *Shabbat* properly, with all its details and nuances. This is indicated in [the verse] "*Tashev enosh*—You turn man back until he is crushed" (Psalms 90:3): *tashev* is the same letters as *Shabbat*,[6] and *enosh* alludes to "[he is forgiven] even if he served idolatry like the generation of Enosh." (*Shabbat* 118b)[7]

---

4. To be mindful of *mitzvot*, and to heed their performance, protects man from sin.

5. To mind God's will by observing His commandments is regarded as "performing kindness with God" (see *Zohar* III:281a, and *Reishit Chochmah*, Sha'ar Ha'ahavah, ch. 8).

6. The Kabbalah teaches that all realms ascend to their spiritual source on the *Shabbat*: they return (*teshuvah*) to their source to be absorbed in higher sanctity (*Eitz Chayim* 40:5 and 8, and 50:6). *Shabbat*, therefore, signifies *teshuvah* on its highest level, and its proper observance, in both the letter and the spirit of the law, effects atonement. This is alluded in the fact that the letters of the word *Shabbat* are the same as of "*tashev*—you turn back; you return."—See also *Keter Shem Tov*, Addenda, no. 118.

7. In the days of Enosh, the grandson of Adam and Eve, "to call in the name of God became profaned" (Genesis 4:26); that is, his generation introduced idolatry (see Maimonides, *Hilchot Avodah Zara*, ch. 1) Proper observance of

c. At the very least be careful with the reading of the *Shema*, recited twice daily, to do so without any alien thought, Heaven forbid.[8] To do so is something inestimably great. This is indicated [in the saying], "Whosoever reads the *Shema* . . . those that cause harm keep away from him." (*Berachot* 5a) "Those that cause harm" refers to all harms in the world, whether they relate to the body or the soul.[9]

You may find it impossible to pray without alien thought; nonetheless, train yourself to commence [reading the *Shema*] without alien thoughts.[10]

---

the *Shabbat*, however, demonstrates *teshuvah*, a return to God, which effects forgiveness even for the grave sin of idolatry.

8. The *Shema* must be read with *kavanah* (concentration on the meaning of the text) and awe. This applies especially to the first two verses ("Hear, O Israel..." and "Blessed is the Name..."); for if these were said without *kavanah*, the duty of the *Shema* has not been fulfilled and it must be read again. (*Shulchan Aruch, Orach Chayim*, sect. 60 and 63)

9. The *Shema* has 248 words (including the three concluding words repeated aloud by the cantor), corresponding to the 248 limbs of the body. With proper recital of the *Shema*, each word effects protection and healing for the limb to which it corresponds. *Tanchuma, Kedoshim*: 6; *Zohar* I:101a; *Zohar Chadash, Acharei*, 48a.

10. In *Likkutim Yekarim*, sect. 198, and other parallel sources, sect. 17-19 appear (with slight variations) as one segment under the heading of "*Tzava'ah* (Testament) of R. Israel Baal Shem Tov."

20

Embrace the trait of *zerizut* (alacrity) very much. Rise from your sleep with alacrity, because you have been renewed and became a different person that is capable to beget, analogous to the attribute of the Holy One, blessed be He, begetting worlds.[1] Whatever you do should be done with alacrity, for you can serve God with everything.[2]

---

1. When man rises from sleeping he is like a new being, as it is written "They are new every morning" (Lamentations 3:23). With the renewed energy, he is able to cause new effects in all realms by means of his worship of God with Torah and *mitzvot*. This is regarded as "begetting" new things, analogous to the Almighty "begetting" (bringing about) all the worlds (*cf. Tikunei Zohar* 69:104a and 105b). Consciousness of this ability should cause one to rise and act with alacrity.

2. The mystics note that laziness, indolence, is rooted in evil, in the realm of impurity. It is evidence of disinterest, and prevents man from worshipping God (*cf.* below, sect. 116). *Zerizut* (alacrity), on the other hand, indicates a desire of the soul and heart to act for the love of God. Thus it is one of the advanced levels on the ladder of spiritual perfection (*cf. Avodah Zara* 20b and its parallel passages).

21

When donning the *talit*[1] one is to see the "blue thread."[2] This means that awe come upon him.[3]

---

1. A four-cornered garment with *tzitzit* (special fringes) attached to each corner (Numbers 15:37*ff.*; Deuteronomy 22:12), commonly called "prayer-shawl."

2. The fringes on all four corners are to contain a *petil techelet*, a thread colored blue (or turquoise) with a dye extracted from an aquatic creature called *chilazon*. (The identity of this creature is no longer known, thus nowadays we are unable to observe that detail of the precept of *tzitzit*.)

   The significance of the *techelet* is that its color reflects the color of the sea, which is similar to that of the sky which, in turn, is analogous to that of the Divine Throne of Glory. Thus "you shall see it and remember all the commandments of God and do them, and you shall not stray after your heart and after your eyes..." (Numbers 15:39) To see the "blue thread" (or, in the present observance, the *tzitzit* in general) is a reminder of God and will prevent man from sinning (*Menachot* 43b; and *cf.* above, sect. 5-6, note 1).

3. The significance of the *talit* is "accepting upon yourself the yoke of the Heavenly Kingdom in the act of spreading the *talit* over your head" (*Zohar* III:120b). The *techelet* signifies the Heavenly Throne of Judgment, thus "you

shall see it and remember all the commandments of God" because of the awe or fear it instills (*ibid.* II:139a and 152a-b; and see also *ibid.* III:175a).

22

Whatever you see, remember the Holy One, blessed be He.[1] Thus [when seeing an aspect of] love, remember the love of God; and with [an aspect of] fear remember the fear of God, as this is elaborated in various sources.[2] Even when going to the privy have in mind "I am separating the bad from the good," with the good remaining for the Divine service. This is the concept of *yichudim* (unifications).[3] Likewise, when going to sleep think that your mental faculties go to the Holy One, blessed be He, and will be strengthened for the Divine service.[4]

1. See above, sect. 2-3 (especially note 3) and 11.
2. Everything in this world has a spiritual root Above. Thus one must trace everything to its Divine root and apply it in that context to the service of God. (*Cf.* above, sect. 13-14, with regard to raising and sublimating all thoughts.)
3. *Cf.* above, sect. 2-3, note 4.
4. See Maimonides, *Hilchot De'ot* 3:3; and above, sect. 20, note 1.

23

Before falling asleep lie in dread and fear, agitated and trembling from the fear of the Creator, blessed be He.[1] Thus you will not come to sin, as it is written, "Be agitated and do not sin, [reflect in your hearts on your beds]..." (Psalms 4:5)[2]

1. When retiring for the night, one should be agitated (tremble) in fear of God (*Zohar* III:113b). It is a time of serious soul-searching and stock-taking (*ibid.* 178b).
2. See above, sect. 9, note 1.

24

Your thought should be [directed] to Above, the Supernal World, in service to God. Cleave unto Him and trust in Him to attain your desire.[1]

---

1. *Cf.* above, sect. 4, and below, beginning of sect. 137. The frequently cited concept that man's thought is to concentrate on the spiritual reality on high is based on the principle that thought is man's very being; thus you are where your thought is (see below, sect. 69).

25

The following is an important principle: Remain all day with the thought with which you rose from your bed, and no other thought.[1]

---

1. Obviously this relates to a thought that is pure in itself or has been sublimated to holiness.

   This sentence can be read also: "One remains all day . . ." (instead of "Remain all day . . .") This would accord with the following teaching of the Baal Shem Tov: Speech and action are rooted in man's thought. If the thought is pure and holy, all subsequent speech and actions, too, will be pure and holy. Thus it is extremely important that the first thought in the morning be proper, for it sets the tone for the whole day. Likewise, one must be careful to "sanctify and purify one's first utterance" every day as one awakens. This requires, however, that one's first thought be attached to holiness. (The Baal Shem Tov explains this in context of the mystical interpretation of the honor due an elder brother, cited below, sect. 90.) See *Keter Shem Tov*, sect. 212, citing *Likkutim Yekarim*, sect. 136.)

26-28

Always be careful to rise at midnight.[1] He who does not rise, without having being prevented beyond his control, incurs a ban Above, Heaven forbid.[2]

---

1. See above, sect. 16.
2. This is based on *Zohar* III:23b (and see there also I:207a).

Convert the nights into days. Sleep a few hours during the day so that you will suffice with but little sleep at night.[3]

When rising at midnight and overcome by sleepiness, drive it away by pacing back and forth in the house and chanting hymns with raised voice.

Study a number of [diverse] subjects. Do not concentrate on a single lesson lest it become onerous for you. Thus study many [different] lessons [and that will banish your sleepiness].

---

3. Sleeping in day-time (except on *Shabbat*) is generally disapproved of, especially by the mystics. If it is necessary to enable one to study Torah at night, however, one may "borrow" from day-time to "repay it" in the night.

29

When you study, pause briefly every hour[1] to attach yourself unto [God], may He be blessed.[2] Even so, you must study.[3]

---

1. "Every hour" is not necessarily to be taken literally. It is a typical Hebrew expression for "every so often."

2. This paragraph, explained in the next one (and elucidated by the much more elaborate parallel-passage in *Likkutei Amarim*–Vitebsk, p. 27b, as well as by sect. 30 below), is no doubt one of the crucial statements in *Tzava'at Harivash*. It offers a succinct declaration of the unique nature of Chassidism and the difference between it and its opponents. The Baal Shem Tov clearly does not downgrade or belittle Torah-study, as often charged by his adversaries. He places Torah-study into context: the ultimate goal of the religious life is *deveikut*—attachment to, and communion with, God.

The Halachic proof-text for this principle is in the Talmudic passage relating that "the pious of old" spent an hour on each of the daily three prayers, and also an hour preparing for each prayer "in order to focus their heart to their Father in Heaven," and an additional hour after each prayer to extend the communion with God beyond the prayer itself (*Berachot* 30b and 32b). Thus they spent nine hours daily on *deveikut* without worrying about the over-riding obligation of Torah-study. For "the goal of wisdom (i.e., the principal purpose of Torah studied) is *teshuvah* (return to, and communion

In the midst of study it is impossible to cleave unto God, blessed be He.[4] Nonetheless one must study because the Torah furbishes the soul and is "a Tree of Life to those who hold fast to it." (Proverbs 3:18) If you do not study, your *deveikut* will cease.[5]

---

with, God) and good deeds" [Rashi: that it be with *teshuvah* and good deeds] (*Berachot* 17b). The precept of authentic *deveikut* with "fear and love of God" is superior to the precept of Torah-study and takes precedence to it, as it is written, "The beginning of wisdom is fear of God" (Psalms 111:10), as stated in *Sefer Chareidim* and in *Shenei Luchot Haberit*. (See the lengthier version in *Likkutei Amarim–Vitebsk*, and R. Schneur Zalman of Liadi, *Shulchan Aruch, Hilchot Talmud Torah* 4:4-5. *Sefer Chareidim, Mitzvat Hateshuvah*, end of ch. 3, writes on the authority of R. Isaac Luria that *deveikut* is sevenfold more effective for the soul than study.) Note, however, the sequel to this sentence.

3. Notwithstanding the primary goal of *deveikut*, it does not over-ride the obligation to study Torah, for the reason explained in the next paragraphs.

4. Torah-study is not a superficial utterance of words. It requires concentration on the content of the subject-matter to the point of full understanding and acquiring *yedi'at Hatorah* (knowledge of Torah). It is practically impossible to do so when simultaneously concentrating on *deveikut* (*cf.* below, sect. 30: "When studying Torah you must concentrate on the subject-matter.") Man thus faces a dilemma: should he pursue meaningful study with its unavoidable interruption of *deveikut*, or focus on *deveikut* at the expense of study and *yedi'at Hatorah*? The Baal Shem Tov's answer is an unequivocal "*you must study!*"

5. "A boor cannot be fearful of sin, and an unlearned person cannot be a *chassid* (a pious person who acts beyond the minimal letter of the law)." (*Avot* 2:5) The lack of Torah-knowledge precludes the possibility of authentic *deveikut*. By not studying Torah, therefore, one loses out on both the basic precept of Torah-knowledge and *deveikut*. As for the "pious of old" (see above, note 1), they spent so much time on prayer and *deveikut* because they had already studied, and already knew the whole Torah. This follows from the Talmud's statement that by virtue of their saintliness "their Torah was preserved." Unlike others, they did not need to spend more time on reviewing etc. to assure that they will not forget what they had learned. Their piety and *deveikut* did not exempt them from the precept of Torah-study, but from the normative obligation of *continuous* Torah-study in accord with

Ponder the fact that you cannot cleave [unto God] when sleeping or when your mind "falls."[6] The time of Torah-study is then certainly not inferior to those conditions.[7] Nonetheless, you must consider at all times attachment to the blessed Creator, as stated above.[8]

---

the Halachic principle (*Berachot* 11a; *Sukah* 25a) that "when preoccupied with one *mitzvah* one is exempt from another *mitzvah*." Thus they continued their studies in the time left to them beyond the nine hours devoted to prayer and *deveikut*. (See at length, *Hilchot Talmud Torah, ibid.*, par. 6)

Note the sentence in sect. 30: "When studying Torah you must concentrate on the subject-matter, and *by virtue thereof you will be properly attached to Godliness.*"

6. I.e., when in a state of constricted consciousness, unable to concentrate and focus.

7. The pursuit of *deveikut* cannot be an excuse not to study Torah. It is a fact of reality that in any case there are times when the active pursuit of *deveikut* is precluded, such as when "the mind falls" (i.e., when unable to concentrate and focus the mind) or when asleep. It is absurd to argue that Torah-study is inferior to those states of being. When studying Torah, at least one fulfills the precept of *talmud Torah* (studying Torah), the precept of acquiring *yedi'at Hatorah* (Torah-knowledge), which is the very foundation of the religious life of following God's will and without which there is no authentic *deveikut*. Thus, "you must study!" Moreover, when the mind is not preoccupied with thoughts of Torah, one is not in a state of *deveikut*, and the mind will be filled with meaningless (*devarim beteilim*—idle matters) or even sinful thoughts (*cf.* below, sect. 121, that the failure to study Torah is one of the four primary causes of spiritual corruption).

8. In view of the above, it is clear that Torah-study is absolutely essential in the full sense of "*Talmud Torah* is equivalent to all the commandments." (*Cf.* below, sect. 117, note 7, and sect. 121.) Nonetheless, every so often one must remind oneself that its pursuit is a command of God, which is part of the service of God and communion with God. *Cf.* below, sect. 54.

30

When conversing think of nothing but attachment to the Creator, blessed is He. When studying Torah, however, you must concentrate on the subject studied, and by virtue thereof you will be properly attached to Godliness.

You must always be occupied with Torah, for it is "a Tree of Life to those who hold fast to it" (Proverbs 3:18). When but conversing and relying on the *deveikut*, however, be very careful not to lapse occasionally from the *deveikut*.[1]

---

1. Torah-study requires concentration on the subject-matter (see above, sect. 29, note 4). You do not lose out on this account, because it is itself the prerequisite for proper *deveikut*. The optional activity of conversing, however, allows for it to be in context of *deveikut*. Any disruption of *deveikut* at that time may reduce it to idle talk and lead astray. *Cf.* below, sect. 81.

31

Something may come your way and you do not know whether to pursue it or not. If you studied Torah that day, however, you will be able to determine your course of action from the subject-matter that you learned.[1] Just assure that you are continuously attached to God; He will then always provide you with the opportunity to know [how to act] from the Torah [studied].[2]

---

1. It is related of the Baal Shem Tov that he would look into sacred texts and then answer those who sought his counsel. In this context note his interpretation of the *Midrash* that states that God concealed the original light of the first day of creation: the light was hidden in the Torah (see *Zohar Chadash*, Ruth, 85a-b; *Sefer Habahir*, par. 147-9), and by means of it one is able to see things that are not normally perceived. (*Degel Machaneh Ephrayim*, on Genesis 1:4)

2. The version of this section in *Likkutim Yekarim* (sect. 11-12) is preceded by the following words: "As you subdue all your thoughts to the Creator, blessed be He, He will inspire your thoughts with [the idea] of what you need to do, as it is said, 'Cast your burden upon God [and He will sustain you.]' (Psalms 55:23). R. Israel Baal Shem Tov said that when you are attached [in a state of *deveikut*] to the Creator, blessed be He, and a thought comes to you about whatever it may be, then things are most likely as it oc-

If, however, one relates to God haphazardly, then God, too, will deal with you in a random way.[3] Moreover, He will not provide you with the garments and food which contain the sparks related to the source of your soul that are meant for you to correct.[4]

---

curred in your thought. This is a bit of *ru'ach hakodesh* (holy spirit; a prophetic spirit)."

3. God relates to man "measure for measure" (*cf.* below, sect. 112. 116 and 142). Thus "if you behave haphazardly with Me, I, too, will deal with you haphazardly" (Leviticus 26:22-24, and see there also verses 21, 27-28, and 40-41).

4. All things in this world contain "holy sparks" that must be elevated to their Divine source. This is achieved by using all things for their intended purpose in context of man's service of God. When permissible foods, garments or objects come your way, it is an indication that they contain "holy sparks" related to your soul, i.e., that it is meant for you to elevate them. (See below, sect. 109.) The punishment for relating to God haphazardly is that you will be deprived of this opportunity.

32

When praying, advance in gradual stages.[1] Do not exhaust all your strength at the beginning of prayer.[2] Commence with composure and in the midst of prayer attach yourself with great *deveikut*. Thus you will even be able to recite the words of the prayer expeditiously.[3]

Though unable to pray with *deveikut* at the outset of prayer, recite the words with great *kavanah* (devotion). Strengthen yourself bit by bit until [God] will help you to pray with intense *deveikut*.[4]

---

1. On the gradual ascent in prayer, see below, sect. 58, 135, and 143.
2. See below, sect. 38.
3. See below, sect. 36.
4. See below, sect. 72, 85 and 86. *Cf.* also sect. 60.

33

You must learn and train yourself to pray with a low voice, even the Hymns [of Praise], and to cry out silently.[1] Whatever you say, whether it be Hymns or [words of Torah-]study, should be said with all your strength, as it is said, "All my bones shall say..." (Psalms 35:10)[2]

An outcry rooted in *deveikut* is silent.

---

1. To pray out loud stimulates *kavanah*. Thus it is customary in many places (and especially among certain schools of Chassidism) to pray loudly, with great intensity (except for the *Amidah* which should not be audible even to those standing next to you). On an elevated level of communion with God, however, when praying with profound focus and devotion in the gripping consciousness of being literally in the very presence of God, the words flow from the very depth of the heart and soul and are practically silent: "Hannah was speaking from the heart, only her lips moved and her voice was not heard." (I Samuel 1:12)

    To pray aloud initially is acceptable, and even necessary, for the average person. Nonetheless, "you must learn and train yourself to pray with a low voice.. and to cry out silently."
2. See below, sect. 34-35, 51, 58, 60, and end of 75.

34

Know that every word is a *komah shelemah*, a complete structure.[1] Thus you must invest it with all your strength, otherwise it will be [defective], like missing a limb.

---

1. Note below, sect. 75: "Every letter contains 'worlds, souls and Divinity.' These ascend and become bound up and united with one another, with Divinity. The letters then unite and become bound together to form a word, becoming truly unified in Divinity ... All worlds will then be unified as one and ascend."

    Below, sect. 118: "When meditating in prayer on all the *kavanot* (mystical devotions) known to you, you are but meditating on those you know. On the other hand, when you say the word with great bonding, all *kavanot* are involved in the whole word of themselves and by themselves. For every letter is a complete world."

Every word of Torah or prayer, therefore, is charged with spiritual forces and signifies the ultimate principle of unity.

35

It is a great kindness of God that man remains alive after praying. In a natural course of events, death would have to result from exhausting all strength [in prayer] because of exerting oneself so much by concentrating on all the great *kavanot* (mystical devotions).[1]

1. See below, sect. 42.

36

Sometimes you can pray very quickly, because the love of God burns very strongly in your heart and the words flow from your mouth by themselves.[1]

1. See above, sect. 32. *Cf. Keter Shem Tov*, sect. 217, that in the state of intense *deveikut*, the holy spark of the *Shechinah* inherent in man's soul will sometimes extend itself to the point that words spoken flow from It. It seems that the person is not speaking by himself but that the words flow from his mouth by themselves.

37

When attaching yourself on high in the silent prayer,[1] you will merit to be raised yet higher during that prayer.[2] Our sages thus said, "He who comes to be purified will be helped." (*Shabbat* 104a)

1. The *Amidah*, which is to be said in an inaudible voice.
2. *Cf.* above, sect. 32.

By means of that prayer you will then merit to be attached on high with your thought.[3] Thus you will attain to the yet greater level of being attached on high even when not engaged in prayer.

---

3. To be attached with your thought is to be attached with your very being, with your soul (*cf.* below, sect. 104). On that level the *deveikut* remains even when not engaged in prayer.

38

Do not recite many Psalms before prayer so that you will not weaken your body. By exerting your strength before prayer with other things you will not be able to recite with *deveikut* the main thing, i.e., the mandatory [prayers] of the day—the "Hymns of Praise," the *Shema* and the *Amidah*.[1]

Thus say first the main thing with *deveikut*. Then, if God gives you additional strength, recite[2] Psalms and the Song of Songs with *deveikut*.

---

1. Some recite Psalms as a preparation for prayer. It helps to focus the mind to the service of prayer: it clears the mind from alien thoughts, and it is condu- cive to *deveikut*. To spend too much time or effort on the preliminary Psalms, however, can be counter-productive, as the energy expended may be at the expense of that required for the mandatory prayers. *Cf. Keter Shem Tov*, sect. 120.
2. At the conclusion of the prayers.

39

On Yom Kippur, before *ne'ilah* (the concluding prayer), recite the *machzor* (liturgy of the day) with *katnut* ("smallness;" limited consciousness) so that you will then be able to pray [*ne'ilah*] with *deveikut*.[1]

---

1. This paragraph is relating the advice of the preceding section to the service of *Yom Kippur*.

40

When you are on a low level, it is preferable to pray out of a *siddur* (prayer book). By virtue of seeing the letters you will pray with greater *kavanah* (devotion).[1]

When attached to the Supernal World, however, it is better to close your eyes, so that the sight [of your eyes] will not distract you from being attached to the Supernal World.[2]

---

1. The mystics emphasize that the letters of the Hebrew alphabet are not conventional symbols for sounds but signify—and are charged with—Divine emanations, lights and creative forces. (*Cf.* below, sect. 75.) The very sight of these holy letters, therefore, stimulates *kavanah*. R. Isaac Luria always prayed out of a *siddur* (except for the *Amidah* which he said with closed eyes).

2. In the state of *deveikut* one does not need the inspiration of seeing the letters and, as stated above, sect. 36, the words will flow of themselves. In fact, in that state, anything else (such as reading the words) will distract.

41

The soul told the Rabbi [the Baal Shem Tov][1] that he did not merit his revelations of supernal matters because he learned so much Talmud and the codifiers, but because his prayers were always with great *kavanah* (devotion).[2] By virtue thereof he merited to attain a high level.

---

1. One of the levels of prophetic spirit is the self-revelation of a person's own soul as it connects with its supernal source. (This form of *ru'ach hakodesh*—holy spirit—is described in R. Chaim Vital, *Sha'arei Kedushah* III:5 and 7.)

2. The Baal Shem Tov was not only a great mystic but also a profound scholar in Talmudic and Halachic studies, as attested by his disciples (many of whom were themselves among the universally acknowledged Torah-scholars and authorities of the time; see the essay by Rabbi S. Y. Zevin in *Sefer Habesht*, Jerusalem 1960, p. 24*ff.*; and the Introduction to B. Mintz's edition of *Shivchei Habesht*, Tel Aviv 1961, p. 19*ff.*) His lectures were not limited to mystical subjects. They included regular lessons in Talmud, the Codes and their commentators, and were delivered with great acuity and

brilliance. He merited his unique revelations, however, by virtue of his extra-ordinary *kavanah* in prayer.

42

Before praying have in mind that you are prepared to die from the *kavanah* (intense concentration) while praying. Some concentrate so intensely that it may be natural for them to die after reciting [just] two or three words before God, blessed be He.[1]

Bearing this in mind, say to yourself: "Why would I have any ulterior motive or pride from my prayer when I am prepared to die after two or three words?"[2]

Indeed, it is a great kindness of God to give [man] the strength to complete the prayer and remain alive.

1. The concentration on every word ought to be to the point that the word is "illuminated and shines" (see below, sect. 75). *Deveikut* to God is by means of attaching one's thought and inwardness to the spiritual core of the letters of Torah and prayer—the spiritual core of the light of the *En Soph* that is in the letters, an "attachment of spirit to spirit." (*Keter Shem Tov*, sect. 44 and 94) Thus when saying a word, you prolong it extensively and do not want to let go of it (below, sect. 70). There is then an intense communion to the point of "my soul yearns, it *expires*, for the courtyards of God" (Psalms 84:3). Thus it may be natural to die (*kelot hanefesh*—expiration of the soul from its pining for God) after reciting but two or three words from the prayer.
2. Prayer with great *deveikut* may lead to a sense of self-satisfaction or other ulterior thoughts. The Baal Shem Tov thus cautions to beware, that the prayer be followed by a profound sense of humility. (See *Darkei Tzedek*, I:no. 5.) *Cf.* above, sect. 12.

43a-b

When fasting,[1] have in mind the following:[2]

1. In line with normative Halachah (Maimonides, *Hilchot De'ot* 3:1; *Shulchan Aruch, Orach Chayim*, sect. 571), Chassidism is opposed to self-

"Woe to me! I have angered the Supreme King on account of my desires and my putrid pride.. That is why I wish to afflict myself to subdue my desires and pride. Thus I will effect Above that "the slave be subservient to his Master and the maid-servant to her Mistress,"[3] and fulfill the precept of *teshuvah*.[4] I wish to afflict myself so that I may serve God truthfully and whole-heartedly, with love and fear, in order that I effect His unity,[5] and also to offer myself as an offering before Him.

"Woe to me! What am I and what is my life? I wish to offer my fat and blood, my body and fire, my spirit, soul, strength,

---

mortifications such as fasting and other forms of self-affliction. It emphasizes that man concentrate on positive forms of self-improvement: "It is preferable to serve God in joy without self-mortifications, because the latter cause feelings of depression" (below, sect. 56). Note also *Likkutim Yekarim*, sect. 178: "The Baal Shem Tov merited all his illuminations and levels by virtue of his constant immersions. Frequent [immersions in a] *mikveh* (ritual pool) is superior to fasting, for fasting weakens the body from the service of God. It is much better to use the energy one would expend on fasting for the study of Torah and prayer, to pray with all one's strength and concentration which leads one to spiritual ascent." (Cited in *Keter Shem Tov*, sect. 219; and see there also sect. 249, 302, and Addenda: sect. 16.)

Nonetheless, fasting is not rejected outright: at times it may be needed for spiritual correction in the context of *teshuvah*. See below, sect. 56; and *cf.* also sect. 76-79.

2. The proper fast is not simply a passive state of "not eating and drinking." It needs be a conscious act with a profound sense of overcoming physical needs and desires in the service of, and submission to, God (see below, notes 4 and 16). This section thus offers the appropriate meditations when fasting.

3. I.e., the subservience of man's natural inclinations to God. *Cf. Tikunei Zohar* 2a.

4. Fasting is not itself *teshuvah* (repentance; return to God), but facilitates the frame of mind required for *teshuvah* (see below, note 16).

5. I.e., the pervasive presence of God as the sole true reality, as opposed to the dualism of the erroneous assumption of a dichotomy between the spiritual and the material.

heart and will before Him.[6] [I want to offer these] to the Creator of all worlds, by whose word all worlds came into being and before whom everything is as nothing—all the more so I, mere dust, a maggot and worm. I cannot but appeal to His great mercies to augment my strength to offer many sacrifices before Him.

"I ought to rejoice so much that I merited to bring [Him] some gratification with my body, spirit and soul. Moreover, I ought to rejoice that He gave us the means to subdue the *yetzer hara* that is upon us.

"I wish to afflict myself because I caused sorrow to the Holy One, blessed be He, and His *Shechinah*,[7] and also to ease that sorrow. Woe to me! Of what significance is my affliction compared to that sorrow which I caused for so many years! I can but appeal to His great mercies to observe my self-affliction to ease the sorrow of His *Shechinah*, and that He remove from us the *kelipot* ('husks;' evil forces) because of my affliction. May I effect Above that all the *kelipot* be removed from the *Shechinah* so that She may be purified and unify with Her 'Spouse,' in absolute unity,[8] in a mode of kindness and

---

6. Fasting diminishes the blood and fat of the body. Thus it is regarded like offering these as a sacrifice on the Divine altar of atonement (*Berachot* 17a). Moreover, fasting involves overcoming the natural desires for food and drink. Thus it implies a sacrifice of not only the physical blood and fat, but more so of soul, strength and will (see *Zohar Chadash*, Ruth:80a).

7. To sin is to cause sorrow to God, on both the level of the Divine Immanence and Presence (*Shechinah*) and the level of the Divine Transcendence ("The Holy One, blessed is He").

8. Sin defiles not only the sinner's body and soul but also, as it were, "covers" the *Shechinah* with the crude husk of evil. The *Shechinah* is thus "exiled" in evil, preventing the manifestation of the Divine Presence. In the metaphorical terminology of the Kabbalah this is regarded as a separation between the *Shechinah* (Divine Immanence) and Her "spouse", the Holy One, blessed is He (Divine Transcendence). Acts of virtue (Torah and *mitzvot*), and specifi-

compassion. My self-affliction will thus effect union from Above to below, from the mind to the heart and from the heart to the liver, and that He pour His effluence upon me as well.[9]

"I trust in Him, for He created all worlds by His word to come into being from nothingness.[10] All is as naught before Him, yet His providence is upon them to endow them with [supernal] effluence and their vitality. Thus surely He can provide me with strength, and in His kindness set His providence upon myself as well, saving me from the *yetzer hara* so that it will not prevent me from my self-affliction by arguing that I am weak and that my mind is withering, and other such enticements.[11] Thus I appeal but to His great kindness, for He put it in my heart to afflict myself. In His kindness He has helped me many times, and this day, too, He will help me, and

---

cally the correction of sin (*teshuvah*), "frees" the *Shechinah* from that exile and reunites Her with Her "spouse."

9. *Zohar* III:153a notes that the Holy One, blessed is He, manifests Himself and His effluence by way of three principal channels which are metaphorically analogous to man's vital organs of the brain, heart and liver. In the human, the liver is the first to absorb nourishment, and it transfers it to the heart which then transfers it to the brain. The order of Divine effluence, however, is in reverse: the aspect of "brain" (the *Sefirah* of *Chochmah*) transfers to the aspect of "heart" (the *Sefirot* of *Ze'eir Anpin*, i.e., *Chessed* to *Yessod*), and the "heart" to the "liver" (the *Sefirah* of *Malchut*) from which it is diffused to the lower levels. When man fasts, he offers "nourishment"—the blood and fat that are diminished in him, and his will—to the supernal "liver," whence it ascends to the supernal "heart" and then to the supernal "brain." The "arousal from below" by man thus initiates a reciprocal "arousal from Above" in the normative order of Divine emanation and effluence.

10. Everything came into being, and continues existing, by means of the ten utterances of the six days of creation (as recorded in Genesis, ch. 1).

11. See below, sect. 78-79.

save me from anything that would prevent me [from my good intentions].

"Moreover, [the fast] is not even an affliction on my part, for everything emanates from Him, blessed be He. On my own I would be altogether unable to afflict myself.[12]

"Thus I submit myself unto Him who created all worlds by means of His word, even to endure all mortifications and disgraces for the sake of His unity. I wish to fulfill 'you shall be holy,' (Leviticus 20:7),[13] and I trust in His kindness that He will augment my strength so that I may serve Him in truth, and that He will help me so that people will not know of my deeds.

"I am not afraid of any weakness on account of the fast, for many people become ill [without fasting]. Moreover, 'the Shechinah sustains the sick, as it is said, 'God supports him upon the bed of illness' (Psalms 41:4).' (Shabbat 12b) Thus, in His kindness, He will surely sustain me.

"Furthermore, 'I am going the way of all the earth' and I will not deviate. Our sages said, 'The greater the person, the greater is his yetzer hara' (Sukah 52a). But as I do not deviate, I can trust in [God]: 'Trust in God and do good' (Psalms 37:3), i.e., one is allowed to trust [in God for the ability] to do Mitz-vot,[14] and 'They that hope in God shall renew strength.' (Isaiah 40:31) Indeed, it is a good omen for one to die while engaged

---

12. Even the strength and energy needed for the fast, man has but by Divine grace. See below, sect. 138, note 1.

13. To be holy means not only to separate from all that is forbidden, but more so to "sanctify yourself by that which is permitted to you," self-restraint in permissible things (see Nachmanides on Leviticus 19:2).

14. This interpretation of Psalms 37:3 (to rely on God to help you fulfill the mitzvot) is identical to that of Nachmanides (Ha'emunah Vehabitachon, ch. 1) and R. Bachaya (Kad Hakemach, s.v. Bitachon).

with *teshuvah*.[15] Without [this *teshuvah*] I may possibly have to be reincarnated because of sin and for having failed to worship properly with love and fear. Also, [it is said] 'Do not worry about the troubles of tomorrow' (*Yevamot* 63b)."

★ ★ ★

The essence of *teshuvah* is to turn back from one's evil ways.[16]

Do not feel proud, for he who takes pride in his fasting "will be delivered to dogs." (*Tikunei Zohar* 18: 33b)[17]

Even "if but a single individual repents, the whole world is forgiven." (*Yoma* 86b) Thus rejoice in the pain of the fast for offering up yourself [to sanctify God's Name], for surely you effected something very great.

[In the days of fasting follow this procedure:]

At the outset sleep in the first three nights—though not too much—in order to strengthen your mental faculties.

Change your place every so often, walk around a bit and then lie down briefly, in order to ease your pain.

Study Torah in your mind, without actual speech, to ease your pain.

Sometimes the mouth feels dry and has a bitter taste, and the *yetzer [hara]* makes it seem to you that your head aches and that it is unbearable for you; but if you trust in the Creator's

---

15. *Cf. Avot deR. Nathan* 25:2: "It is a good omen for one to die whilst engaged with a *mitzvah*."

16. *Cf. Ta'anit* 16a: "Neither sackcloth nor fastings are effective, but only *teshuvah* and good deeds, as we find that it is not said of the people of Ninveh that God saw their sackcloth and fasting, but, 'God saw their *deeds*, that they turned from their evil way' (Jonah 3:10)." Fasts serve the purpose to stir the heart to *teshuvah*, the essence of which is to turn from one's evil ways and return to God (see Maimonides, *Hilchot Ta'anit* 5:1).

17. *Cf.* below, sect. 77.

kindness your vigor will be strengthened, and there is no pain at all.[18]

Have in mind that your fast is to bring gratification unto the Creator, blessed is He, and that you accept the pain upon yourself in order to ease the pain of the *Shechinah*. Worship with joy, and have in mind that the *Shechinah* sustains you even as She sustains others that are ill, and then God will help you.

---

18. See below, sect. 78-79.

44

Sometimes the *yetzer hara* deceives you by telling you that you committed a grave sin when there was really no sin at all or [at worst you violated] a mere stringency. His intent is that you should feel depressed as a result thereof, and thus be kept from serving the Creator, blessed be He, because of your depression.

You must understand this trickery, and say to the *yetzer hara*: "I will not pay attention to the stringency you referred to. You speak falsely, for your intent is but to keep me from His service, may He be blessed. Even if there really was a degree of sin,[1] my Creator will be more gratified if I do not pay attention to the stringency that you pointed out [to me] to make me depressed in His worship.

"In fact, I will serve Him with joy! For it is a basic rule that I do not think the Divine service to be for my own sake but to bring gratification to God.[2] Though I ignore the stringency you mentioned, the Creator will not hold it against me, because I do not pay attention to it only so that I will not be kept

---

1. See below, sect. 46, note 2.
2. See above, sect. 11, and below, sect. 47.

from His service, blessed be He. For how can I negate His service, even for a moment!"

This is a major principle in the service of the Creator, blessed be He: avoid depression as much as possible.[3]

---

3. *Cf.* below, sect. 45 and 107. This whole section (and the similar one below, 46) requires elaboration. It was often cited by the opponents to Chassidism as "proof" of anti-nomianism. To read it that way, however, is a total distortion.

The Baal Shem Tov does not belittle sin or the remorse it requires. He interprets Isaiah 19:1, "Behold, God rides on a light *av* (cloud)": God dwells with that person who regards any sin he committed to be *av* (thick; coarse) even if it is essentially a *light* transgression. (*Keter Shem Tov*, sect. 398)

Here (and below, sect. 46) he cautions against the psychological effects of obsessive remorse that leads to depression. To be depressed by one's spiritual deficiencies or downfall may seem laudable, but it is really counterproductive. As already stated by R. Chaim Vital (the principal disciple of R. Isaac Luria, and the authoritative scribe of his teachings), *atzvut* (depression; melancholy) is a nasty, harmful and objectionable character-trait that is a hindrance to the service of God, (see *Sha'arei Kedushah* I: 2 and 5; II: 4; III: 4; *Sha'ar Ru'ach Hakodesh*, p. 33b; and the quote cited below, sect. 107, note 2). Thus it must be avoided altogether.

Remorse for sin is necessary. It is part of *teshuvah*. But this *mitzvah* of *teshuvah* must be separated from the observance of the other *mitzvot*. There is a specific time for everything. When the obligation or opportunity of *mitzvot* comes about, one must pursue it with alacrity and joy, setting aside all other matters, and in particular the concern about one's spiritual status. Think of God and not yourself!

"Turn away from evil and do good." (Psalms 34:15) R. Dov Ber of Mezhirech, disciple and successor of the Baal Shem Tov, interpreted: When it comes to Torah-study and service of God, you must put aside all other thoughts, such as thoughts of self-reproach for past misdeeds or personal worthlessness, for these are but the device of the *yetzer hara* to prevent you from your present obligation. Thus "turn away from (real or imagined) evil," i.e., forget now these thoughts, "and do good," i.e., carry out your obligations in proper manner with joy and eagerness. (*Or Hame'ir, Shabbat Teshuvah*)

In fact, this principle is an established premise of much earlier authorities: "A person must never think to himself 'I am a sinner and committed many transgressions; thus of what avail is it for me to perform *mitzvot*?' On the contrary: if he has committed many sins, he should countermand that with the performance of *mitzvot*. Thus it is stated in *Vayikra Rabba* [21:5]: 'For with *tachbulot* (wise advice) you shall wage your war' (Proverbs 24:6); i.e., if you have committed bundles (*chabilot*) upon bundles of transgressions, countermand them by bundles upon bundles of *mitzvot*." (R. Israel ibn Al-Nakawa, *Menorat Hama'or, Perek Hamitzvot*, p. 394f.; and see also R. Menachem Me'iri, *Chibur Hateshuvah* I:ch. 12)

This accords with the Talmudic proverb, "If one has eaten garlic so that his breath smells, should he eat more garlic so that his breath should go on smelling?" (*Shabbat* 31a) In other words, we do not say to a wicked person, "Be still more wicked and abstain from *mitzvot*." This principle is applied on the practical level of Jewish law (see Maimonides, *Hilchot Tefilah* 15:6).

Abundant joy in the performance of all *mitzvot* is itself mandated by Halachah, as it is written "Serve God with joy, come before Him with joyous song" (Psalms 100:2), and as ruled categorically by Maimonides in his Code, *Hilchot Lulav* 8:15.

The Baal Shem Tov's teaching here, and below, sect. 46, thus offers guidance that preserves and strengthens Halachic observance. It follows an earlier ruling by R. Eleazar Azkari: "Though a person may be depressed on account of his sins, he must be joyful at the time of Divine service, as it is written, 'Because you did not serve God, your God, with joy and gladness of the heart.' (Deuteronomy 28:47) This applies to every service of God, and how much more so then to the service of prayer which is called 'the service of the heart' (*Ta'anit* 2a)." (*Sefer Chareidim*, Mitzvat Hateshuvah, ch. 4)

45

Weeping is very bad because man must serve [God] with joy.[1] Weeping that results from happiness, however, is very good.[2]

---

1. See above, sect. 15 and 44, and below, sect. 107.
2. *Zohar Chadash* (Ruth:80a) notes that there is a good kind of tears and a bad kind of tears. The good kind is brought about by the *yetzer tov* and ascends on high. This includes when a person in distress sheds tears in prayer, placing his trust in God and seeking His mercy and compassion to remove the anguish (see below, sect. 107, note 2). More so it includes tears of remorse in context of *teshuvah*, which indicate the sincerity of ultimate *teshuvah* (see

Zohar Chadash, ad loc.). Another kind of positive (and commendable) weeping is the one mentioned here, i.e., the one that results from overwhelming joy, or the ecstatic state of *deveikut*, as when tears flowed from R. Akiva's eyes when hearing the mystical meanings of the Song of Songs (*Zohar* I:98b).

Other kinds of weeping are at least suspect. Tears of anger and frustration, or in prayers for evil to come upon another, are not received by God (*Zohar Chadash, ad loc.*). Moreover, R. Chaim Ibn Atar notes that weeping (beyond the "good" types referred to above) may be the symptom of resignation, signifying a lack of faith in God (*Or Hachayim*, Numbers 11:18). For true faith and trust in God must of itself lead to joy and gladness (*Reishit Chochmah, Sha'ar Ho'ahavah*, ch. 12). Thus beyond the moment of distress, or the appropriate times for prayers of penitence, one's service of God must be with joy. See below, sect. 107, note 2.

This section offers a general principle on its own, but gains clarification when read in context of the sequence of sections 44-46.

46

[As you set out to serve God,] do not be overly punctilious in all you do.[1] [To do so] is but a contrivance of the *yetzer*

---

1. Note carefully the qualifying admonition of the Maggid of Mezhirech: "Our minds are not as powerful as those of the earlier [generations], thus we are unable to follow properly all *chumrot* (stringencies of the law). [Preoccupation with these would cause] a cessation of *deveikut* because of our weak mind, unlike the earlier ones whose mind was very powerful.

   "Even so, one must be very careful in this matter and weigh actual practice on the scales of the mind: if the stringency will cause a negation of *deveikut* between himself and the Creator, it is better not to be overly stringent. However, this applies only to *extra* stringencies that man *undertakes on his own*. As for the *chumrot* that are stated explicitly in *Shulchan Aruch*, one must observe these even if it appears in his mind that to do so will negate the *deveikut*. He is surely wrong [in that assumption]. For the Torah in its totality, including all its details, precautionary measures and subtleties, from the [time of the] Faithful Shepherd (Moses) up to [and including] the *Shulchan Aruch*, was given to us solely to become attached to His great Name by means of the deeds we do. [That includes] even the precautionary laws [that are Rabbinic]. Thus it is said in a general way: 'Even what a conscien-

[hara] to make you apprehensive that you may not have fulfilled your obligation, in order to make you feel depressed.
Depression, in turn, is an immense obstacle to the service of
the Creator, blessed be He.

Even if you did commit a sin, [Heaven forbid], do not be
overly depressed lest this stop your worship. Do feel saddened
by the sin [and feel ashamed before the Creator, blessed be
He, and beg him to remove your evil]; but then rejoice in the
Creator, blessed be He, because you fully repented and re-
solved never to repeat your folly.

Even if you are certain that you did not fulfill some obligation, because of a variety of obstacles, do not feel depressed.
Bear in mind that the Creator, blessed be He, "searches the
hearts and minds" (Psalms 7:10). He knows that you wish to
do the best but were unable to do so. Thus strengthen yourself
to rejoice in the Creator, blessed be He.[2]

It is written, "There is a time to act for God, they voided
Your Torah." (Psalms 119:126) This implies that the performance of a *mitzvah* may sometimes entail an intimation of sin.[3]
In that case do not pay attention to the *yetzer hara* who seeks to
prevent you from performing that *mitzvah*. Respond to the *yet-*

---

tious student will innovate in the future [was said already to Moses at Si-
nai]' (*Yerushalmi, Pe'ah* 2:4; see *Megilah* 19b and *Vayikra Rabba* 22:1), and 'the
Torah and the Holy One, blessed is He, are entirely one' (see below, sect.
54, note 1). One must be careful, though, that it is done exclusively *lishmah*
(for its own sake) without, Heaven forbid, associating any personal delight;
for that would be very base, as stated by the saint, the author of *Chovot Halevovot* (*Sha'ar Yichud Hama'aseh*, ch. 1-4), see there." (*Likkutei Amarim*, from
the manuscript of R. Menachem Mendel of Vitebsk, p. 29a-b)

2. On these first three paragraphs see also above, sect. 44, and the notes there.
3. See the interpretation of this verse in *Berachot* 63a. Note there also the refer-
    ence to "In all your ways acknowledge Him" (Proverbs 3:6), i.e., even for a
    matter of transgression; and see on this Maimonides' *Mishnah*-Commentary
    on *Berachot* 9:5, and his *Shemonah Perakim*, end of ch. 5.

zer [hara]: "My sole intent with that *mitzvah* is but to bring gratification to the Creator, blessed be He." With the help of God the *yetzer hara* will then depart from you. Nonetheless, you must carefully determine in your mind whether or not to perform that *mitzvah*![4]

All that I have written[5] are important principles "more desirable than much fine gold." Each item is an important principle.

---

4. I.e., this is a very serious matter. You cannot simply follow your impulse with all the best of intentions in context of what is stated here. The decision to proceed in such circumstances requires careful consideration.
5. The wording ("I have written") indicates that this last paragraph is an addition by the editor of the manuscript, for the author did not record his teachings.

47

"Many did like R. Shimon bar Yochai, but they were not successful." (*Berachot* 35b)

This means that they wanted to subject themselves to many self-mortifications in order to attain the level of R. Shimon bar Yochai. That is why they did not succeed.[1]

When serving God, have in mind nothing but to bring gratification to the Creator, blessed be He, and not the attainment of [high] levels.[2]

---

1. The emphasis of our text is a condemnation of ulterior motives: a self-serving pursuit of "the level of R. Shimon bar Yochai" will not succeed. Elsewhere the Baal Shem Tov adds a warning: in trying to attain that level you are over-reaching your own level and capacity, naively emulating others to attain something that is beyond you. To do so, however, is counter-productive. For a) you will not obtain what you seek, and b) you will lose what you had already! (*Keter Shem Tov*, sect. 4, citing *Ben Porat Yossef*, Foreword; and the parallel-passages in *Toldot Yaakov Yossef*, Mikeitz:1 and Metzora:1. Cf. *Moreh Nevuchim* I:34.)
2. See above, sect. 11.

48

When you see that your worship excels that of another, do not be arrogant. Thus it is said , "One is not to say [in his heart], 'I am greater than my fellow.'" (*Oti'ot deR. Akiva, s.v. Dalet*)[1]

---

1. See above, sect. 12.

49

Another important principle: When people ridicule you about your worship, whether it be with regard to prayer or other matters, do not respond.[1] Do not reply even in a positive way, so that you will not be drawn into quarrels or into haughtiness which causes one to forget the Creator, blessed be He.[2] Our sages said that "man's silence leads him to humility."[3]

---

1. "The practice of the righteous is to suffer insult and not to insult, to hear themselves reviled without answering." (Maimonides, *Hilchot De'ot* 2:3, based on *Shabbat* 88b.)
2. Haughtiness leads to forgetting your Creator, as it is written "Your heart becomes haughty and you will forget God, your God" (Deuteronomy 8:14; see *Sotah* 5a).
3. See R. Chaim Vital, *Sha'arei Kedushah* II:5.

50

Do not gaze at the face of people whose thoughts are not continuously attached to the Creator, blessed be He, even when speaking to them; for that gaze will blemish your soul.[1]

---

1. This is an extension of the Talmudic admonition not to gaze at the face of a wicked person (*Megilah* 28a) In the same context one should not use books written by wicked people, even if they contain sacred texts (see R. Judah Hachassid, *Sefer Chassidim*, sect. 249; R. Dov Ber of Mezhirech, *Maggid Devarav Leya'akov*, sect. 52).

As for fit people however, i.e., those whose thoughts are attached to the Creator, blessed be He, you ought to gaze at them and thus accrue holiness to your soul.[2]

---

2. This whole section follows upon the principle that one is affected by what one sees, especially when gazing with intent. See above, sect. 5-6, and note 1 there.

51

Torah-study must be with intensity[1] and great joy.[2] This will diminish alien thoughts.[3]

---

1. I.e., with all your strength and energy. *Cf. Eruvin* 54a, that for Torah-study to be effective and retained one must clearly utter the words with the mouth. Moreover, one's whole being should be involved, for "if it is 'ordered' in your 248 limbs it will be secure, but if not it will not be secure."
2. All *mitzvot* must be performed with joy (see above, sect. 44, and note 3 there). This applies even more so to Torah-study, as explained below, sect. 119.
3. "Alien thoughts" relates to any kind of sinful, idle or distracting thoughts. Intensive and joyful Torah-study helps to overcome these, as it is said, "He who takes to heart the words of Torah will have negated for himself many mental preoccupations.. foolish preoccupations, unchaste preoccupations, preoccupations with the *yetzer hara* . . . preoccupations with idle things." (*Avot deR. Nathan*, ch. 20) "Our sages thus declared that man should direct his mind and thoughts to the words of Torah and enlarge his understanding with wisdom, for unchaste thoughts prevail only in a heart devoid of wisdom." (Maimonides, *Hilchot Issurei Bi'ah* 22:21, based on *Kidushin* 30b and *Midrash Mishlei*, ch. 24).

52

When one serves God every moment, there is no opportunity to be arrogant, to love pride or other character-traits that are evil.[1]

---

1. See above, sect. 10, and sect. 51, note 3.

53

Regard yourself as nothing, as the *Gemara* (*Sotah* 21b) interprets the verse "Wisdom shall be found from 'nothing.'" (Job 28:12)[1]

This means that you are to regard yourself as if you are not in this world,[2] thus "what is there to gain from people esteeming you?"[3]

---

1. "Words of Torah remain only with him who makes himself as one who is nothing, as it is written, "Wisdom shall be found from nothing."

2. I.e., material reality and pursuits mean nothing to you: you are indifferent to them and you concentrate solely on the spiritual. See below, sect. 62.

3. *Cf.* above, sect. 2, 5-6 and 10.

54

When studying Torah bear in mind in whose presence you learn.[1] It may happen that in your study you may be removed from the Creator, blessed be He; thus you must give serious consideration [to this matter] at all times.[2]

---

1. See below, sect. 119, that God is "concentrated," as it were, in the Torah. "The Torah and the Holy One, blessed, is He, are entirely one," as the *Zohar* states: "The Holy One, blessed is He, is called Torah.. and the Torah is but the Holy One, blessed is He" (II:60a); "the Torah is literally the Name of the Holy One, blessed is He.. and He and His Name are one" (*ibid.* 90b).

2. See above, sect. 29-30, and the notes there.

55

When desirous to perform a *mitzvah*, make every effort to do so. Do not allow the *yetzer hara* to dissuade you by saying that to do so may lead you to pride. You make sure to do it anyway.[1]

---

1. The Baal Shem Tov continuously emphasizes the need for observing *mitzvot* with *kavanah* (proper intent), with love and fear of God, with *deveikut*.

Nonetheless, be very careful: if a sense of pride arises in you in the midst of fulfilling [the *mitzvah*], push it away with vigor and enthusiasm.[2] No doubt but that ultimately you will act literally *lishmah* (for [the *mitzvah's*] own sake) without any sense of pride, for "out of *shelo lishmah* (doing it "not for its own sake") comes *lishmah* (doing "for its own sake").(*Pesachim* 50b)

Do as many *Mitzvot* as you can, and the Holy One, blessed is He, will help you to act without ulterior motives.[3] You must, though, strengthen yourself to the best of your ability.[4]

Nonetheless, he recognizes an objective validity to the very act of a *mitzvah*. Thus he states that one is to do them even if the ideal consciousness is as yet lacking (just as we saw earlier, sect. 29-30, that he demanded Torah-study even when presently deficient of the sense of *deveikut*).

Underlying this teaching is the principle that one must beware of the wiles of the *yetzer hara*. It does not simply try to seduce man to do outright evil. Oftentimes it will appear as a "pious saint" demanding optimum spirituality and belittling religious behavior that is not up to that par. The *yetzer hara* is intent to prevent man from his religious obligations and spiritual involvements by proposing misleading arguments of hypocrisy, unworthiness, and so forth (see below, sect. 74 and 117, and the notes there). Thus one is to ignore these arguments and to do as many *mitzvot* and good deeds as one can, even if they may not yet be on the ideal level of *lishmah* (for its own sake). Note carefully the more detailed restatement of this section, below, sect. 126, and the Baal Shem Tov's teaching in *Keter Shem Tov*, sect. 393. *Cf.* also below, sect. 91.

Here, again, we have a clear refutation of the accusations of antinomianism by the opponents of the Baal Shem Tov and Chassidism.

2. In other words, do not refrain from performing the *mitzvah* but battle the negative thoughts that would prevent you from it.
3. It is an established principle that he who seeks sincerely to be purified will be helped by God to achieve his goal (*Shabbat* 104a).
4. All that has been said above is not an excuse to simply go through the motions of the *mitzvot* mechanically, as by rote, even when thinking that eventually it will be done properly. "You must strengthen yourself to the best of your ability" to observe the *mitzvot* in ideal fashion.

56

If you feel a desire to fast, be careful not to negate that desire.[1] Indeed, you know that it is preferable to serve God in joy, without self-mortifications, because the latter cause feelings of depression.[2] Nonetheless, it may be assumed that you know of yourself that you need to fast because you did not yet correct your soul properly.[3]

[In this context bear in mind that] there are many things about which some need be very scrupulous and accept upon themselves various stringencies, because of the state of their soul, while others need not be that scrupulous.[4]

---

1. See above, sect. 55, and the notes there, and note 3 below.
2. See above, sect. 43, note 1.
3. Normative Halachah forbids arbitrary self-affliction. It is allowed (within certain limits) in context of *teshuvah* or other forms of spiritual self-correction (see commentators on *Shulchan Aruch, Orach Chayim*, sect. 571; *Shulchan Aruch Harav, Orach Chayim* 155:1, and *Choshen Mishpat, Hilchot Nizkei Haguf*: par. 4).
4. See Maimonides, *Hilchot De'ot*, ch. 2, and his *Shemonah Perakim*, ch. 4.

57

Before praying have in mind that you are prepared to die from the *kavanah* (concentration) during the prayer. Some people concentrate so intensely that it may be natural for them to die after reciting [just] two or three words before God, blessed be He.

Bearing this in mind, say to yourself: "Why would I have any ulterior motive or pride from my prayer when I am prepared to die after two or three words?"

Indeed, it is a great kindness of God to give me the strength to complete the prayer and remain alive.[1]

---

1. This section is a duplication of above, sect. 42; see there.

58

There is "a flaming sword that revolves to guard the path to the Tree of Life." (Genesis 3:24)

When a person wishes to attach his thoughts to the supernal worlds, to the Creator, blessed be He, the *kelipot* ("husks;" forces of evil) will not let him. Nonetheless, in spite of the obstacle, you must force yourself with all your strength many times in one and the same prayer and attach yourself to the Creator, blessed be His Name. Thus you will enter the supernal worlds.[1]

Strengthen yourself in believing, with perfect faith, that "the whole earth is full of His glory" (Isaiah 6:3)[2]—and this is when you are in the Supernal World. Thus it is written, "The righteous lives by his faith." (Habakuk 2:4)[3]

Even if you may have fallen from your level in that prayer, recite the words with lesser *kavanah* (concentration) to the best of your ability, and then strengthen yourself to return to your level. Do so even if this may happen several times with that same level. At first say the "body" of the word, and then invest it with its soul.[4]

At first you must bestir yourself with your body, with all your strength, in order that the power of the soul shine forth in you.[5] Thus it is said in the *Zohar* (III:166b and 168a) that a

---

1. I.e., do not be discouraged by the obstacle. Keep trying as hard as you can and eventually you will succeed. See the parable below, sect. 72 and 86.
2. See below, sect. 84 and 137.
3. Again, do not be discouraged by your "fall," but gradually work your way up again. *Cf.* above, sect. 32.
4. The word *per se* is like the body, a vessel. Man's *kavanah*, the proper thought and concentration when reciting the word, infuses it with its soul. In the gradual ascent, first recite each word, and then contemplate on its meaning and significance. *Cf. Keter Shem Tov*, sect. 17 and 284.
5. *Kavanah* can be induced by physical activity of the body. One way is to pray (initially) with raised voice (see above, sect. 33, note 1). Another way is

wooden beam that will not burn should be splintered and it will become aflame. Afterward you will be able to worship with the mind alone, without any movements of the body.[6]

---

bodily movements, swaying to and fro during prayer (*Shulchan Aruch, Orach Chayim* 48:1; and see below, sect. 68).

Ideally one should reach a stage of *deveikut* in which the prayers are recited in an undertone and immobile in the consciousness of standing before God (see above, sect. 33, and below, sect. 104-105; *Keter Shem Tov*, sect. 226). Nonetheless, "when a person is drowning in a river, and gesticulates in the water to extricate himself from the waters that sweep him away, observers will surely not laugh at him and his motions. So, too, one should not mock him when he tries to save himself from the 'evil waters'—i.e., the *kelipot* and alien thoughts which come to prevent him from having his mind on his prayer." (*Keter Shem Tov*, sect. 215)

6. See above, sect. 33, and below, sect. 59 and 104-105.

59

Sometimes, when you are attached to the Supernal World, to the Creator, blessed be He, you must guard yourself against any movements, even with the body, so that your *deveikut* (attachment) will not cease.[1]

---

1. See above, sect. 58, notes 5-6. In the state of *deveikut*, physical reality is transcended. Conscious movements, therefore, would be disruptive and counter-productive to *deveikut*.

60-61

It is impossible to pray with *kavanah* (devotion) without exertion.[1] You must entreat God for help and assistance.[2]

---

1. The Talmud (*Berachot* 32b) states that prayer requires vigor or exertion, i.e., that one must always strengthen himself, with all his energy.

2. "At the beginning (of the *Amidah*, the essential prayer) one has to say 'God, open my lips and my mouth shall declare Your praise' (Psalms 51:17)." (*Berachot* 4b) The reason is to entreat God for help and assistance to be able to pray properly (see R. Samuel Edelis, *Chidushei Aggadot, ad loc.*; R. David

Consider that it is to your benefit when God helps you to have complete *kavanah* for half or most of your prayer. If, in the end, you feel weak and the *deveikut* is lost, what can you do? Pray to the best of your ability with lesser *kavanah* until the end of *Aleinu* [i.e., the concluding prayer].[3]

Abudraham. *Abudraham, s.v. Shemonei Esrei*; and *cf.* Nachmanides, *Ha'emunah Vehabitachon*, ch. 5. *Cf.* also *Maggid Devarav Leya'akov*, sect. 146, cited in *Keter Shem Tov*, sect. 400.) As stated earlier, one may place his trust in God to enable him to do *mitzvot* (above, sect. 43, and note 14 there), and God will indeed help him (above, sect. 55, note 3).

3. *Cf. Zohar* I:243b: "[R. Chizkiyah asked:] 'What of a person whose heart is troubled and he wishes to pray, or he is in distress and unable to recount the praises of his Master?' [R. Yosse] answered him: 'He may not be able to concentrate his heart and mind, but why should the order of his Master's praises be diminished? He is to recount the praises of his Master in spite of his inability to concentrate, and then pray.'"

62

"If I am not for myself, who is for me? [And if I am for myself, what am I?..]." (*Avot* 1:14)

When praying one must be like divested from physical reality, unaware of your existence in this world.[1] That is to say, "When I reach the level that I am altogether unaware whether I am in this world or not, I will certainly have no fear of alien thoughts. For when I am divested of this world, alien thoughts

1. *Shulchan Aruch*, Orach Chayim 98:1.—The Baal Shem Tov defines this: no longer to sense the feelings of the body and this world; all worldly desires—let alone evil character-traits—are despised in one's heart and eyes, and are totally meaningless in view of one's longing for the Creator. Your thoughts are but on the supernal worlds, on the spiritual reality underlying everything, and you vest your mind and soul into these thoughts. (*Keter Shem Tov*, sect. 199, 239 and 284; and see there also sect. 240 and 279.)

will not approach me."[2] This is the meaning of "who is for me?," i.e., what alien thought will come to me?

But "If I am for myself," i.e., when I regard myself as something substantial and real in this world, then I am really as of no value at all. This is the meaning of "what am I?," i.e., of what significance am I, and of what value is my service before God? For then alien thoughts will disturb me and I am as nothing in this world. The principal purpose of man's creation in this world is service [of God];[3] but I am unable to perform His service because alien thoughts disturb me.[4]

---

2. In the state of self-negation (*cf.* above, sect. 53) he is indifferent to worldly concerns and desires. Moreover, as he reduced himself to naught, he is unassailable by alien thoughts or negative forces.
3. *Kidushin* 82a
4. See also the shorter version of this section, below, sect. 97.

63

When you want to seclude yourself [with God],[1] a companion should be with you. It is dangerous to do so alone. Two people should be in the room, each one secluding himself on his own with the Creator, blessed be He.[2]

At times, when attached [to God], you can practice solitude even in a house full of people.[3]

---

1. See below, sect. 82, that *hitbodedut* (meditation in seclusion) is an effective way to attain *deveikut*.
2. See, though, *Keter Shem Tov*, sect. 216, that the pursuit of *deveikut* beyond the periods of prayer is better in total seclusion, "that no other person be there; for even the chirpings of birds can interfere, as also the thoughts of another."
3. In the state of *deveikut* one is oblivious to all surroundings.

64

Sometimes one may fall from his level on his own, because God knows that you need this. At other times this fall
may be caused by the environment. The "descent", however,
is for the sake of an "ascent," i.e., to reach a higher level.[1] Thus
it is written, "He will guide us *al muth* (lit., to death)." (Psalms
48:15)[2] It is also written, "And Abram descended to Egypt"
(Genesis 12:10) and "Abram ascended from Egypt" (Genesis
13:1):[3] Abram signifies the soul (*Zohar* I:122b), and Egypt signifies the *kelipot* ("husks;" forces of evil)[4]

---

1. By attaining spiritual levels one may feel content with that achievement. He
    does not realize that he has not yet reached his full potential. Thus he will
    "fall" to a lower level. This will surely cause him to be disturbed, thus moti-
    vate him to make a greater effort to regain his loss and attain yet higher
    levels. See below, sect. 67, note 1.
2. Degradation, i.e., reduction in rank, is tantamount to death (*Tanchuma*, Vay-
    echi:2; *Zohar* III:135b: "The term death applies to anyone who was lowered
    from the earlier level he had"). Thus "He will guide us to death," i.e., to re-
    duction in rank, in order that we make an effort to ascend higher.
    Others (*Targum*, Rashi etc.) read *al-muth* as one word which means
    "youth; childhood." Still others (see Ibn Ezra) read the one word *almut* to be
    derived from *helem*, concealment. These two readings converge in the Baal
    Shem Tov's interpretation of this verse with a parable of a father teaching
    his child to walk: every time the child takes two or three steps toward the
    father, the father distances himself in order to make the child walk further.
    So, too, God is the "hiding God" (Isaiah 45:15) in order that one come yet
    closer to Him. (*Kedushat Levi* on Exodus 3:11; more extensively in *Turei Za-
    hav, Rimzei Rosh Hashanah*; and briefly in *Keter Shem Tov*, sect. 237.) There is
    then a "fall" for man, a concealment of God, in order that he bestir himself
    to greater ascents.
3. God tested Abraham: right after telling him to move to the Holy Land, and
    promising him every manner of blessing, He caused a famine in the land
    which forced Abraham to *descend* to Egypt. This ordeal was a test of Abra-
    ham's faith, whether or not he would question the original command and
    promises (*Tanchuma, Lech*: 5; quoted by Rashi).

A test (*nisayon*) is meant to *elevate* the person: "*lenasot*—in order to test you" (Exodus 20:17), i.e., to elevate and magnify you (*Mechilta, Bachodesh*: ch. 9, quoted by Rashi; *cf. Zohar* I:140a, and below, sect. 132).

Abraham did not waver in his faith, thus "Abram *ascended* from Egypt," returning enriched both spiritually and materially. *Cf. Keter Shem Tov*, sect. 27 and 151.

4. "What is the meaning of 'Abram ascended from Egypt'?..When the soul is saved from that 'evil officer'... the 'king of Egypt,' that is, the king of the oppressors that distress the souls, i.e., the destructive angels, the demons ... what is written of the masters of the soul? 'Abram *ascended* from Egypt'! He is raised beyond them, with great strength—he, his soul and all his possessions." (*Zohar Chadash, Tikunim*:118c)

65

You must perform your deeds in a concealed manner, so that people will not note your piety. But before you reach a high level you must act openly.[1] Otherwise, if you act openly like [the rest of] the world, and only inwardly seek to be pious, you may be drawn to become like [the rest of] the world.[2] Your [good] intention of *lishmah* (for its own sake) may thus

1. The concealed form of worship is a sign of sincerity. It shows that man thinks but of God alone, and is indifferent to being recognized or esteemed by others for his good deeds (see below, sect. 122). This section cautions, though, that before being able to choose this path you must first assure that you have reached a high level of thorough training and commitment to act properly.

2. A person is influenced by his deeds and actions. This is a continuously repeated principle in *Sefer Hachinuch* (e.g., sect. 16, 31, 40, 95, 99 etc.), and already discussed earlier at length by Maimonides (*Shemonah Perakim*, ch. 4). To pretend to be a simpleton, by acting in the unrefined manner of the masses before attaining a high level, may condition a person to become like them. The best intentions, therefore, will prove counter-productive.

The Baal Shem Tov thus cautions that you must first prove yourself with normative religious behavior, scrupulous commitment to Halachah, before trying to become a "secret" or "hidden" saint.

result in [the very opposite thereof, that it is done] *shelo lishmah* (not for its own sake).[3]

---

3. "One should always occupy oneself with Torah and *mitzvot* though it is yet *shelo lishmah* (not for its own sake; with ulterior motives), for out of *shelo lishmah* one will [eventually] come [to doing it] *lishmah* (for its own sake; without any ulterior motives)." (*Pesachim* 50b; see above, sect. 55, and below, sect. 126.) There is, though, also the danger, as in the presently stated condition, that "out of doing it *lishmah* one may come to act *shelo lishmah*."

66

When you wish to pray, first bring yourself to a state of awe,[1] for it is the gate to enter before God.[2] Say in your heart: "To whom do I wish to attach myself? To the One who created all worlds by His word, gives them existence and sustains them."

Contemplate His greatness and exaltedness, and then you will be able to enter the supernal worlds.[3]

---

1. Fear, or reverence, of God.
2. "'Fear of God is the beginning of wisdom . . .' (Psalms 111:10). 'This is the gate to God' (Psalms 118:20), for surely without entering that gate one will never gain access to the Supreme King . . ." (*Zohar* I:7b; and cf. *Shabbat* 31b)
3. The state of fear or awe is attained by contemplating God's majesty, His great and wondrous works and creations, and realizing one's own insignificance. (Maimonides, *Hilchot Yessodei Hatorah* 2:1-2 and 4:12) This contemplation is a prerequisite to prayer when one must be aware "before whom you stand" (*Berachot* 28b), i.e., "to think of the exaltedness of God and the lowliness of man" (*Shulchan Aruch, Orach Chayim* 98:1).

67

Sometimes a person worships in a state of *katnut* ("smallness;" limited or restricted consciousness):[1] he does not enter

---

1. Man's consciousness cannot always concentrate on the ideal level of sublime *deveikut*. It goes through stages of ebb and flow, "*ratzo veshov*—running (ad-

the supernal worlds at all. His thought, however, is directed to [the fact that] "the whole earth is full of His glory" (Isaiah 6:3), and that he is close to [God].[2] In that state he is like a child whose mind is but slight and not yet developed. Nonetheless, though worshipping on a level of *katnut*, he does so with great *deveikut*.[3]

vancing to absorption in spirituality) and returning (recoiling to mundane reality)" (Ezekiel 1:14). There are "falls" (descents) from the state of *gadlut* ("greatness;" expanded consciousness) to *katnut* that may come about by one's own doing or as part of the natural phases through which the soul passes. These are not necessarily failures: they may happen (a)in order that the soul "regenerate" itself, as it were; or (b) as a "descent for the purpose of subsequent ascent" (see above, sect. 64). In fact, they are in principle unavoidable: it is impossible to remain in a constant state of ideal *deveikut*, because that *deveikut* would then turn into something common and natural and would not be appreciated—for "continuous delight ceases to be delight" (see below, sect. 111, and *Keter Shem Tov*, sect. 121). At the same time, however, this does not mean that *deveikut* itself has to cease altogether: there is an ebb and flow from one stage to another, as explained here, further on.

2. Even in the state of *katnut* one can easily remain conscious of the omnipresence of God, thus also one's own closeness to God at all times.—See below, sect. 137.

3. "Even when you 'fall' from your level. remain attached to the Creator albeit with a small thought.. By virtue of that *katnut* you can come to *gadlut*. Thus we see that if there remains a single spark among coals it can be blown up to become a great flame." (*Likkutim Yekarim*, sect. 171; *Keter Shem Tov*, sect. 217) The aforementioned consciousness of Divine omnipresence is itself a degree of *deveikut*, albeit on the level of *katnut*. See also below, sect. 69.

68

Prayer is *zivug* (coupling) with the *Shechinah*.[1] Just as there is motion at the beginning of coupling, so, too, one must

1. The words of prayer must be articulated (*Berachot* 31a; *Zohar* III:294b). The words, however, are merely the *body* of prayer; its essence or soul is *kavanah*, the mental involvement and concentration (see above, sect. 58). Prayer is

move (sway) at the beginning of prayer. Thereafter one can stand still, without motion, attached to the *Shechinah* with great *deveikut*.[2]

As a result of your swaying, you can attain great bestirment. For you think to yourself: "Why do I move myself? Presumably it is because the *Shechinah* surely stands before me." This will effect in you a state of great *hitlahavut* (enthusiasm; rapture).

"deep calling unto deep," the depth of man's heart and soul seeking union with, and absorption in, its ultimate root and source, i.e., the *Shechinah*. Prayer thus expresses the soul's longing for Divinity ("My soul thirsts for You, my flesh longs for You." Psalms 63:3), "being bonded to the love of God, continuously enraptured by it like the love-sick whose mind is never free from his passion.. as Solomon expressed it allegorically (Song 2:5) 'I am sick with love.'" (Maimonides, *Hilchot Teshuvah* 10:3) In the metaphorical terminology of the Kabbalah, therefore, prayer is "*zivug* with the *Shechinah*" (see *Zohar* II:200b and 216b; cf. *Keter Shem Tov*, sect. 16 and 362).

2. See above, sect. 58-59, and below, sect. 104-105.

69

You may be in a state of *katnut* ("smallness;" restricted consciousness) with great attachment to the *Shechinah*.[1] If, however, you will then think of the Supernal World, you will instantaneously be in the upper worlds.[2] For a person is where his thought is.[3] Thus if you had not been in that upper world, you would not have thought of it at all.

---

1. See above, sect. 67.
2. Thus you can ascend from *katnut* to *gadlut*.
3. Man is identical with his thought (*Tikunei Zohar* 21:63a, and *Zohar* III:247b). Man himself, therefore, is where his thoughts are. (This oft-cited concept of the Baal Shem Tov appears also in a modified version: "Wherever the person's *will* and thought are, that is where he is himself." *Keter Shem Tov*, Addenda, sect. 38, note 42.)

70

Deveikut means that when saying a word you prolong that word extensively. By virtue of *deveikut* you do not want to let go of that word and, therefore, draw it out.[1]

---

1. See *Keter Shem Tov*, sect. 44 and 192. Note *Maggid Devarav Leya'akov*, sect. 46-47 (*cf. Keter Shem Tov*, sect. 284): "When praying.. place your whole thought into the power of the words you articulate until you perceive how the [Divine] lights in the words become enkindled from one another, thus generating various lights. The lights of the letters are 'chambers' of God into which He draws His emanations." The concentration on the words, therefore, leads to unity with their inherent Divinity: a state of *deveikut*, attachment and cleaving unto God that one does not want to let go of.

71

If you have an alien thought when praying, *kelipah* ("husk;" forces of evil) is riding on [your] utterances, Heaven forbid; for thought rides upon the [words of] speech.

This is the meaning of "[My love, *dimitich* (I compare you)] to a horse in the chariot of Pharaoh." (Song 1:9) Words are referred to as horses.[1] When Pharaoh, i.e., the alien thought,[2] rides upon them, then "my love, *dimitich*": it is better to be silent.[3]

---

1. The words and letters of the Torah and prayers are compared to "horses" (*Tikunei Zohar* 8a; *ibid.* 5:20b and 47:84b): they are the "vehicle" subservient to, and guided by, the rider (the soul; man's thoughts and mind), taking him to places he is unable to reach on his own (see *Maggid Devarav Leya'akov*, Addenda, sect. 7).
2. Pharaoh signifies *kelipah*, the evil mind and alien thoughts opposed to holiness. *Cf.* above, sect. 64, note 4.
3. The Baal Shem Tov interprets *dimitich* as an idiom of the root-word *damam* (to keep silent). The proof-text thus reads: if the "horse" (the words of prayer) is in the chariot of Pharaoh (i.e., alien thoughts ride it), then *dimitich*—I silence you, my beloved (it is better to stop praying until that impediment is removed).

On the other hand, "words that come from the heart enter the heart,"[4] i.e., [they enter] the heart of Above, by means of the breath, as is well known.[5]

---

4. A popular proverb stated in *Sefer Hayashar* (attributed to R. Tam), Sha'ar 13; cited in *Shenei Luchot Haberit*, Sha'ar Ha'otiot, *s.v.* lev tov, (p. 50b).
5. Breath comes from exhaling, of which the *Zohar* states that "he who exhales, exhales from within himself," i.e., from his inwardness, his innermost vitality. Words that ascend are those which are formed by the "exhalation" rooted in the very core of man's heart, i.e., uttered with *kavanah* and fervor.

72

Sometimes, when [you feel that you are] unable to pray, do not believe that you are definitely unable to pray that day. Strengthen yourself all the more[1] and the awe [of God] will come upon you ever more.[2]

This is comparable to a king who sets out to wage war and disguises himself. Those who are wise recognize him by his mannerisms. Those who are less wise recognize the king by noting the place with extraordinary guarding: surely that is the place of the king.[3]

Thus it is when you are unable to pray with *kavanah*. You must know that there is additional guarding all around the King. The King is there, but you are unable to approach Him because of the special protection surrounding Him. Thus fortify yourself with awe, great strength and additional *kavanah*, so that you will be able to come close and pray before God. You will then be able to pray with exceeding *kavanah*.

---

1. See above, sect. 58 and 60-61.
2. Awe of God is a prerequisite for proper prayer (above, sect. 66).
3. This parable is cited again below, sect. 86; see there.

73

"One should not rise to pray but with *koved rosh* (lit., "heaviness of the head;" humility)." (*Berachot* 30b)

This means: do not pray for that which *you* lack,[1] for then your prayer will not be acceptable.[2] If you wish to pray, do so for the sake of the "heaviness in the Head." For whatever you lack, that same deficiency is in the *Shechinah*, [as it were].[3] For man is a "part of God from on high."[4] Any deficiency in a part, therefore, applies to the Whole as well, and the Whole senses the deficiency of the part.[5]

---

1. He who does not pray daily for sustenance is of little faith (*Zohar* II:62a-b). To beseech God for our constant needs is an expression of our belief in God and Divine Providence, an acknowledgment of Divine sovereignty and our continuous dependence on God for everything we have and require. Nonetheless, this concept must be placed in the wider context of ultimate reality where events and conditions on earth reflect spiritual "events and conditions." This section explains this wider context and its implications.

2. I.e., it is not the ideal prayer. Emphasis on personal desires, let alone presumptuous "calculation on prayer" (*iyun tefilah*), i.e., expecting that God will grant these desires as compensation due for praying, may be counterproductive: it causes a celestial "audit" of the supplicant's record, thus draws attention to his sins and failures (see *Berachot* 32b; *Rosh Hashanah* 16b; and the commentaries *ad loc.*)

3. The *Shechinah* is referred to as "Head" (see *Zohar* III:187a). *Koved rosh*, in its literal meaning of "heaviness of the head," would thus refer to the afflictive heaviness of the *Shechinah*. This is the anthropomorphic concept of Divine pathos, the sufferings the *Shechinah* shares with man, that appears frequently in Talmud and Midrash (*Sanhedrin* 46a; *Mechilta* on Exodus 12:41 and 17:15; *Sifre* on Numbers 10:35; *Midrash Tehilim* 20:1; and the numerous parallel passages), essentially based on Isaiah 63:9 and Psalms 91:15. Deficiencies and suffering on earth, therefore, reflect, as it were, an analogous condition Above, in the *Shechinah*.

4. Job 31:2. The *Shechinah* is the very root and source of all souls (*Zohar* I:25a; *Tikunei Zohar* 3b). Every soul is a spark or "limb" of the *Shechinah* (*Zohar* III:17a and 231b).

5. The lifeless (i.e., soul-less) body does not feel pain or sense any needs. By implication, then, suffering is sensed by the soul (the "limb" of the *Shechi-*

Your prayer, therefore, should be for the deficiency in the Whole.[6] This is the meaning of "but *mitoch koved rosh* (because of the 'heaviness in the Head')."

---

nah), not the body. If the pain or deficiency is sensed by the part, by the individual extension of the *Shechinah*, it is sensed also by the "Whole," by the *Shechinah per se.*

6. Prayer on behalf of the *Shechinah* (the "Whole") of itself covers the problems or needs of man (the part of the "Whole"); for "as his prayer is answered and 'Salvation is [wrought] unto God (i.e., the *Shechinah*),' this brings about also the conclusion of that verse that 'Your blessing is upon Your people, Selah' (Psalms 3:9)." (*Likkutim Yekarim*, sect. 123; and see also *Maggid Devarav Leya'akov*, sect. 53.)

In this context the Baal Shem Tov resolves two contradictory passages: one (cited above, note 1) states that one must pray daily for personal needs; the other (*Tikunei Zohar* 6:22a) refers to those who pray for their personal or material needs as "arrogant dogs, barking *hav hav*—give us food"! The Baal Shem Tov explains: One may, indeed *must*, pray for all and any needs, if for no other reason but the acknowledgment and consciousness of Divine sovereignty and every thing's total and continuous dependence on God. Nonetheless, one is not to lose perspective: do not get carried away by transient details instead of concentrating on the whole. (*Degel Machaneh Ephrayim*, Likkutim)

Even so, the Baal Shem Tov cautions: "The worker of deceit shall not dwell in My house, he who tells lies has no place before My eyes." (Psalms 101:7) Thus when overcome by the anguish of personal needs and unable to rise above this, *never pretend* to pray for the sake of the *Shechinah*. God examines the heart and knows the truth. Better to be honest and pray for yourself than the falsehood of pretending concern for the *Shechinah*! (*Keter Shem Tov*, sect. 395)

74

"The words of his mouth are evil and deceit; he has ceased to be wise, to do good." (Psalms 36:4-5)

There are two types of [wicked] people. The first is altogether wicked, "he knows his Master yet purposely sets out to rebel against him."[1]

The second one is blinded by the *yetzer hara* and imagines himself to be altogether righteous, and also appears as such to people. He may study Torah continuously, pray and afflict himself. In truth, however, his effort is all for naught, because he lacks attachment [*deveikut*] to the Creator, blessed be He, as well as the perfect faith that is required for constant attachment unto Him, blessed be He. He is unaware of the essential form of worship that is required for proper [Torah]-study and prayer, and to perform a commandment *lishmah* (for its own sake).

The difference between these [two] is as follows:

The altogether wicked one can be cured from his affliction: when he is bestirred by the sense of *teshuvah* and returns to God with all his heart, begging God to show him "the way where light dwells" (Job 38:19).

For the second one, however, there is no remedy. His eyes are bedaubed from seeing the Creator, blessed be He, His greatness, and how to worship Him. He is righteous in his own eyes; thus how can he return with *teshuvah*?

Thus when the *yetzer hara* seduces man to commit a sin, he will make it appear to him as though he has performed a *mitzvah* so that he will never repent.[2]

---

1. A Midrashic expression for one who brazenly acts wickedly (*Sifra*, Bechukotay, cited by Rashi on Genesis 10:9).

2. The *yetzer hara* disguises himself as *yetzer tov*, as an advocate for good, to entice man. He approaches each one on his own level. Simple people he leads to blatant sins. Torah-scholars, who might not succumb to blatant sin, he leads to sanctimoniousness by urging them to study Torah and perform *mitzvot* in an inappropriate way. Their sense of self-righteousness thus precludes them from *teshuvah*. See below, sect. 117; *Keter Shem Tov*, sect. 78 and 114. *Cf.* above, sect. 55, and the notes there.

This is alluded in the verse "The words of his mouth[3] are evil and deceit": the *yetzer hara* deceives a person by making it seem to him that his transgression is a *mitzvah*. Thus "he[4] has ceased to be wise, to do good," i.e., he has left off from ever repenting, as stated above.[5]

More serious yet, "he devises evil on his bed" (Psalms 36:5).[6] That is, [the *yetzer hara*] deceives him further as follows: when he falls [ill and is] bedridden, he prays to God to heal his illness by virtue of the Torah and *Mitzvot* he had performed. He does not realize that this only recalls his sins.[7] All this is the enticement of the *yetzer hara*.

---

3. I.e., the words of the *yetzer hara*.
4. The victim of the *yetzer hara*.
5. See below, sect. 117, for a similar interpretation of our proof-text. See also below, sect. 124, for another emphasis on the pitfalls of self-righteousness.
6. The verse following immediately upon our proof-text.
7. Man's expectation that God grant his wishes as compensation due for his merits, "recalls his sins" by drawing celestial attention to, and a review of, his spiritual record and status (*Berachot* 32b and *Rosh Hashanah* 16b). Quite clearly this will not be to his benefit. (*Cf.* above, sect. 73, note 2.)

75

R. Israel Baal Shem [Tov], peace be upon him, said:

"Make a light for the *teivah* (ark) [and finish it to (the width of) an *amah* (cubit) on high . . .]." (Genesis 6:16) This means that the *teivah* (word)[1] should shine. [This will be understood by the following:]

Every letter contains "worlds, souls and Divinity."[2] These ascend and become bound up and united with one another,

---

1. *Teivah* also means "word."
2. Every word is a "complete structure" (above, sect. 34), every letter a "complete world" (below, sect. 118). Every letter harbors *Or Ein Sof* (a light of the Infinite), which is its individual aspect of *Shechinah* (Divine Indwelling).

with Divinity. The letters then unite and become bound together to form a word [*teivah*], becoming truly unified in Divinity. Man, therefore, must include his soul in each of these aspects.[3] All worlds will then be unified as one and ascend, and this effects immeasurably great joy and delight.[4]

This is the meaning of "[make it with] bottom, second and third [stories]" (*ibid.*), referring to "worlds, souls and Divinity;"[5] [for "The Holy One, blessed is He,] has three worlds [in which He is concealed]" (*Zohar* III:159a [6]).

The *or* (light), however, needs a *keli* (vessel) to contain it. Moreover, as the (relatively) finite *keli* is to contain the infinite *or*, there is need for an intermediary to bring them together, to make it possible for the *or* to be contained in the *keli*. This intermediary is referred to as *neshamah* (soul). Thus each letter compounds *olamot* ("worlds;" i.e., the "vessels"), *neshamot* ("souls;" i.e., the intermediary faculties), and *Elokut* ("Divinity;" the Divine lights). [This is the Baal Shem Tov's terminology for what R. Isaac Luria refers to as "*orot* (lights)-*nitzotzim* (sparks)-*keilim* (vessels);" R. Chaim Vital, *Eitz Chayim, Sha'ar* XIX. See *Keter Shem Tov*, Addenda, sect. 175.]

3. See above, sect. 42, note 1.

4. This whole paragraph appears also (nearly verbatim) in the Baal Shem Tov's famous letter to his brother-in-law, R. Abraham Gershon of Kitov; see *Keter Shem Tov*, sect. 1, p. 1b. It is cited also, with elaboration, by the Baal Shem Tov's grandson and disciple R. Mosheh Chaim Ephraim of Sydilkov, in *Degel Machaneh Ephrayim, No'ach.*

5. The bottom floor refers to the aspect of "Worlds;" the second one to the aspect of "Souls;" and the third (upper) one to the "Divine Lights." See *Degel Machaneh Ephrayim, No'ach.*

6. See there the commentary of R. Mosheh Zaccuto that these are (a)the first "world" (level) of Divine concealment which is referred to as *Adam Kadmon*, (b)the second level of Divine concealment which is referred to as the World of *Atzilut*, and (c)the third level of ever-increasing concealment, compounding the Worlds of *Beri'ah, Yetzirah* and *Assiyah*. [*Shenei Luchot Haberit*, Parshat No'ach (p. 276; in current editions, p. 9*df.*), relates the three levels in the ark to the individual Worlds of *Beri'ah, Yetzirah* and *Assiyah*.]

an attendant

With every word you must hear what you say, because it is the *Shechinah* [Herself], the "World of Speech," who speaks,[7] provided that [the word] has a "light," i.e., that it emerges with brightness[8] and to bring gratification to your Maker. This requires great faith, as the *Shechinah* is referred to as "true faithfulness" (Isaiah 25:1; see *Zohar* I:22a and III:16b).[9] Without faith, it is, Heaven forbid, a case of "he that murmurs separates the Master [of the universe]." (Proverbs 16:28)[10]

[The concluding phrase] "finish it to an *amah* (cubit) on high" means "to *imah* (the 'mother')."[11]

---

7. The term "world(s)" in Kabbalistic and Chassidic thought does not refer to geographic areas but to a spiritual realm, level or category. Man's soul is a spark or "limb" of the *Shechinah* (see above, sect. 73, note 4). When that soul was infused into the body of the original human, "man became a *nefesh chayah* (lit.: a living being)" (Genesis 2:7), which *Targum Onkelos* and *Targum Yehonathan* translate: "*ru'ach memalala—a speaking* spirit" (see Rashi and Nachmanides on this verse). Human speech is a manifestation of the soul, thus rooted in the *Shechinah*. The *Shechinah*, therefore, is referred to as the "World of Speech" (see *Zohar* III:228b and 230a; and *cf. Zohar Chadash, Bereishit*:10d).

8. I.e., that you make a light for the word, you make it shine brightly (as stated above, in the first paragraph), by uttering it in proper manner.

9. I.e., you must be conscious with true faith of the presence of, and relationship with, the *Shechinah*.

10. It causes a separation between the "Master of the Universe" (the Holy One, blessed is He; the aspect of Divine transcendence) and the *Shechinah* (the aspect of Divine immanence); *Zohar* III:31a; *Tikunei Zohar* 2b and 5a. [See above, sect. 43, notes 7-8, on the concepts of the unity and separation between the aspects of Divine transcendence and Divine immanence.]

11. "Finish it (i.e., raise the prayer) to *imah*."

  The Kabbalistic term *ima* (mother) is synonymous with *Shechinah*. The Kabbalah, however, speaks of *imah* on two levels, i.e., two levels of the Divine manifestation that is called *Shechinah*: (a)*imah ila'ah*, the supernal "mother" (supernal *Shechinah*), which in the sphere of the *Sefirot* corresponds to *Binah*; and (b)*imah tata'ah*, the lower "mother" (lower *Shechinah*), which corresponds to the *Sefirah* of *Malchut*. General reference to *Shechinah*,

Alternatively one can interpret as follows:

Once the word has left your mouth there is no need to mind it any more. That is, one does not see it ascend to the higher realm, just as one is not able to look at the sun. This is the meaning of "finish it on high."[12]

---

and especially in terms of "World of Speech," relates to *imah tata'ah*, the *Sefirah* of *Malchut*.

The speech of prayer, therefore, is on the level of the "lower *Shechinah*." As the prayer is infused with true devotion (*kavanah*) it ascends on high to the "supernal recess" (the *Sefirah Binah*; the "supernal mother" or "supernal *Shechinah*") "whence issue all blessings and all freedom to sustain everything" (*Zohar* I:229a). Thus, "Meritorious is the mouth that by prayer provides a resting-place for the *Shechinah*, as it is said 'you make the *mother* lie down (rest) between the lips' (Psalms 68:14; interpreting the word *im* (if) to read *eim* (mother)—see *Tikunei Zohar* 18:34a), i.e., to make the 'supernal mother' rest between them." (*Zohar Chadash, Tikunim,* 101d) This is the ultimate conclusion of prayer, "finish it to the *imah*, on high."

12. The principal prayer (the *Amidah*) starts with the verse "A-D-N-Y (My Lord), open my lips and my mouth will declare Your praise" (Psalms 51:17). The term *A-D-N-Y* signifies the lowest *Sefirah (Malchut)*, thus the "lower *Shechinah*", the World of Speech. ["Prayer is speech.. it is the *Shechinah*, it is *A-D-N-Y*.. The mystery of speech is '*A-D-N-Y*, open my lips ...;" *Tikunei Zohar* 2b, and see also *Zohar* III:228b.] The same prayer concludes with the verse "May the words of my mouth and the meditations of my heart be to *ratzon* (find favor) before You, God." (Psalms 19:15). *Ratzon* signifies the highest *Sefirah (Keter)*. When praying we raise the words of the prayer from *Malchut* (the World of Speech) to *Binah* (the World of Thought), whence they ascend further on their own. (R. Joseph Gikatilla, *Sha'arei Orah,* end of *Sha'ar* II) Thus "you do not (need not; indeed are unable to) see it ascend to the higher realm" which, in any case, is beyond our grasp. "We raise the World of Speech to the World of Thought. The brightness there is very great . . . analogous to the sun which we are unable to gaze at because of its intense brightness." (*Maggid Devarav Leya'akov,* sect. 160; cited in *Keter Shem Tov,* sect. 400.)

One can achieve this by "Come into the *teivah*, you with all your family" (Genesis 7:1), i.e., with all of your body and strength.[13]   *beitecha*

---

13. I.e., by concentrating on the words of prayer with your whole being, body and mind. *Cf.* above, sect. 33-34 and 60-61.

76

[A teaching] of R. Israel Baal Shem [Tov]:

"For My thoughts are not your thoughts, neither are your ways My ways." (Isaiah 55:8) This means: the moment you separate yourself from God, you are worshipping idolatry.[1] There is no middle ground. This is the meaning of "you turn astray and you serve [other gods]." (Deuteronomy 11:16)[2]

Nonetheless, the Talmud states (*Makot* 23b) that "he who refrains from committing a transgression, it is accounted to

---

1. I.e., the moment you separate yourself from your *deveikut* (attachment; bond) with God, it is as if you serve 'other gods.' God is the sole true reality; everything is continuously dependent on God for its very existence. To ignore this principle, to forget the obligation of "Acknowledge Him in all your ways" (Proverbs 3:6)—i.e., even in all your personal and physical pursuits and engagements (Maimonides, *Hilchot De'ot* 3:3; *Shulchan Aruch, Orach Chayim*: 231)—is like denying this principle and setting up an authority or power independent of God, and this is tantamount to idolatry. [R. Menachem Nachum of Czernobyl notes that the Baal Shem Tov would frequently cite this interpretation of Deuteronomy 11:16. (*Me'or Einayim, Shemot*)]

   The Baal Shem Tov thus reads our proof-text: "When your thoughts are not My thoughts (i.e., they are not bound to God, *then*) your ways are not My ways (i.e., the way of God, or worship of God)." (*Cf. Maggid Devarav Leya'akov*, sect. 228.]

2. I.e., the moment "you turn astray"—"you serve other gods."

him as if had performed a *mitzvah*." This is the meaning of "your ways are not My ways."[3]

---

3. The last sentence may be a summary of the general principle stated in the first paragraph (as rendered above, note 2 "for then 'your ways are not My ways'"). Then, again, it may relate specifically to the second paragraph by interpreting it "and not your ways, *but* My ways": when you overcome the temptation to commit a transgression, thus "not [following] *your* ways," it is accounted to you as if you had performed a *mitzvah* (i.e., it is "*My* ways.").

77

When you fast, even if it be from one Shabbat until the next, do not harbor ulterior thoughts, even the slightest. Do not say in your heart that you are doing something great by afflicting yourself that much, and that the fasting will greatly purify you.[1] Rather think to yourself: "Of what esteem are my deeds compared to the service of the angels whose service of God is constant? I am but a 'putrid drop'[2] and my end is unto dust!"

---

1. See above, sect. 43, on the proper meditations when fasting. Ulterior mo-tives, let alone a sense of self-satisfaction in thinking to have attained spiritual heights and perfection, are the very anti-thesis of Divine worship (see above, sect. 11-12). Indeed, "If you fasted from one *Shabbat* to the next, and at the end of the last day your harbored an ulterior motive . . . you have lost all the good stored for you from your fast and your effort was for naught." (*Maggid Devarav Leya'akov*, sect. 196) The parallel-passage of this section in *Likkutim Yekarim*, sect. 188, thus adds here: "This fast goes to the *sitra achara*" (the "other side," the side opposed to holiness).

2. *Avot* 3:1

78-79

In the middle of the week[1] the *yetzer hara* will sometimes over-power you, by making it seem to you that your fasting is

---

1. When fasting a whole week, from one *Shabbat* to the next.

very difficult for you, and saying that you are unable to bear it.[2] Understand that the *yetzer [hara]* is envious of you, lest you attain a [higher] level.[3] That is why he instigates so much against you.

If you are wise and over-power the *yetzer [hara]*, you will effect something great on high. Thus it is said in the *Zohar* (II:128b and 184a), "The glory of the Holy One, blessed is He, is increased when that *sitra achara* (other side; the side of evil) is subdued for the sake of His service." The *yetzer [hara]* greatly desires to prevent you from fasting; but as you over-power him, the *sitra achara* is very much subdued.[4]

The *yetzer hara* is sometimes allowed to cause you great pain. This happens to test you whether you will persist and over-power the *yetzer hara*. [If you do so, you will note] afterwards, at the conclusion of the fast, that you no longer sense the great pain you felt at the time.

Beseech the mercies of the Creator, blessed be He, to strengthen your eyes so that they will not be affected adversely by your fasting.[5]

---

2. See above, sect. 43, text relating to note 11.
3. This does not imply that you should have in mind the attainment of a higher level, for that would be counter-productive (as stated above, sect. 77, and *cf.* sect. 47). Rather, the *yetzer hara* does not want you to acquire the purification for which you felt a need in context of *teshuvah* (return and attachment to God), and which prompted you to undertake the fast.
4. See above, sect. 9.
5. See above, sect. 43.

80

Sometimes you need to gaze in different directions in order to attach your thought to the Creator, blessed be He. This is necessitated by the materiality of the body which is an obstructing barrier to the soul.[1]

---

1. The materiality of the body can be overcome by diffusing it. Gazing in different directions will break the body's concentration on any of its physical pursuits. *Cf.* above, the last paragraph of sect. 58.

81

An important principle:

Attach yourself to the Creator, blessed be He, and in that state of attachment pray for some need of your household, or do or say something though there is no need for that act or speech. Do so in order to train yourself to have your thought attached to the Creator, blessed be He, even when you are involved in actions or speech relating to material matters, to become accustomed to a state of *deveikut* at that time.[1]

---

1. The ideal service of God is not by separating yourself from the world and physical reality. On the contrary: the latter must be sublimated to holiness, the principle of "Acknowledge Him in all your ways" (Proverbs 3:6; see above, sect. 11, note 1, and 76, note 2; below, sect. 94). This, however, is a precarious and hazardous task. Thus you must work your way into it. The advice given here is to train yourself into that frame of mind by gradually introducing mundane involvements during the "safe" times of *deveikut*. This will acclimate you to the reverse: you will be able to invoke *deveikut* during times of mundane involvements. *Cf.* below, sect. 140.

82-83

One merits *deveikut* by *hitbodedut* (seclusion) from people,[1] by writing "secrets of the Torah,"[2] and by performing the *yi-*

---

1. *Cf.* above, sect. 63. The principle that *hitbodedut* is conducive to *deveikut* is stated already in *Reishit Chochmah, Sha'ar Ha'ahavah*, ch. 3 and 10.

2. Profound deliberation in Torah leads to *deveikut* (*Reishit Chochmah*, ibid., ch. 4 and 10). This would then apply especially to *razei Torah*, the mystical meanings of the Torah, which are called *nishmata de'orayta* (the soul of the

chudim (acts of unification) known from R. Isaac Luria, of blessed memory.[3]

When performing *yichudim*, meditate on God's greatness to the best of your ability.

Also, be scrupulous in rising at midnight[4] and to join the day and the night [with Torah and prayer].[5]

Torah; *Zohar* III:152a, and *ibid.* 79b and II:55b). The concealed aspect (soul) of the Torah connects with the concealed aspect (soul) of man, and binds it to the "concealed aspect of the Holy One, blessed is He" (see *Zohar* III:73a).

3. See above, sect. 3, note 4. The teachings of R. Isaac Luria offer the meditations to effect *yichudim*.

4. See above, sect. 16 and 26-27. Torah-study at night is especially conducive to *deveikut* (*Reishit Chochmah, ibid.*, ch. 10).

5. The mystics are very emphatic on the special virtue in joining the night to the day (in the morning) with Torah and prayer (see R. Chaim Vital, *Sha'ar Hakavanot, Derushei Halailah*, ch. 4; *Reishit Chochmah, Sha'ar Hakedushah*, ch. 17). *Shenei Luchot Haberit* (cited by *Magen Avraham, Orach Chayim* 1:1) states that this applies also to joining the day to the night (in the evening).

84

Sifra (*Shemini*) states: "Remove the *yetzer hara* from your heart . . . As [God] is singular in the world, so, too, your service must be singularly [devoted] to Him."

This is an important principle. Man must always have but a singular thought in the service of the Creator, blessed be He.[1] Thus it is written, "God made it that they will fear Him" (Ecclesiastes 3:24) and "[God has made man upright,] but they sought out manifold contrivances" (*ibid.* 7:29); that is, your manifold thoughts cause you to be confused.[2]

---

1. I.e., the thought of devoting himself to the service of God. *Cf.* Maimonides, *Hilchot Shemitah Veyovel* 13:13.

2. "'God has made man upright, but they sought manifold contrivances,' and these contrivances bring the evils upon him." (Maimonides, *Moreh Nevuchim* III:12)

Have in mind that everything in the world is filled with
the Creator, blessed be He. Everything that comes about
through the thoughts of man with various devices, even the
most trivial thing happening in the world, it is all by His
providence, blessed be He.[3] Thus it should make no difference
to you whether your aim was achieved as you wished or not.
As everything comes from the Creator, you know that it is best
for you when things did not happen as you wished.[4]

Bear in mind that everything, whether it be the World of
the Spheres, the World of the Angels or the World of the
Throne,[5] all is as naught before Him, blessed be He. For all
are within the vacated space of His constricted light, of His
Self-contraction,[6] and everything came into being by means of
a single utterance.[7] Why, then, should you be drawn after
anything desirable in those worlds when all is but a single utterance of [God]? It is better to attach yourself beyond the

---

3. Without the Divine effusion and vitality, man is unable to make any motion
    (*Likkutim Yekarim*, sect. 54; *Keter Shem Tov*, sect. 200). In that sense, then, it
    can be said that "the Creator is in every motion, and it is impossible to make
    any motion or (utter) any speech without the ability conferred by the
    Creator. This, indeed, is the meaning of 'the whole earth is filled with His
    glory' (Isaiah 6:3)." (*Maggid Devarav Leya'akov*, sect. 38; *Keter Shem Tov*, sect.
    273.)
4. See above, sect. 2 and 4. See also below, sect. 137.
5. The Worlds of *Assiyah, Yetzirah* and *Beri'ah*, respectively.
6. The concept of *tzimtzum*, i.e., of the Divine "Self-contraction" that con-
    cealed the infinite light to make it possible for finite beings to exist without
    becoming nullified by the intensity of the infinite light of God.
7. *Zohar Chadash, Midrash Hane'elam*:2d.—The world was created with ten
    utterances (*Avot* 5:1). The Talmud comments: The phrase "He said" ap-
    pears only *nine* times in the account of the creation? The term *Bereishit* (In
    the Beginning; the very first word of the Torah) is also an utterance (thus to
    be added to the other nine). (*Rosh Hashanah* 32a) Moreover, *Bereishit* is a
    comprehensive utterance which compounds all the others, and out of which
    all the others follow (*Zohar* I:15a-b, 16b, 30a and 31b.)

worlds, to that which is primary, i.e., to the Creator, blessed be He, than becoming attached to something that is subordinate.[8]

This is what the *Zohar* (II:134b) means by stating: "happy are the righteous who know to fix their will upon the Supernal King, and not upon this world and its vain desires;" for all the worlds are destined to destruction.[9]

Thus always bear in mind to attach yourself to the Creator, blessed be He, with a complete love that is greater than that for anything else in the world; for every good thing in this world is rooted in Him, blessed be He. Think [to yourself]: "I always wish to bring gratification unto [God], and to serve Him constantly." Your thought should always be attached to the Supernal World, to [God].[10] This is alluded in the meaning of the verse, "he shall not leave the Sanctuary." (Leviticus 21:12)[11]

When you have to speak at length about mundane matters, think to yourself that you are descending from the Supernal World to below. Be as one who leaves his house for the outside with the intent to return right away, thinking throughout his departure "when can I return home?"[12] So, too, even when you speak of mundane matters, always think of the Supernal World, for there is your primary abode with the Creator,

---

8. *Cf.* below, sect. 87, 90 and 101-b.

9. *Sanhedrin* 97a. The mystics generally agree that this is not meant in the literal sense, but refers to the destruction of all negative aspects and the universe being renewed on a sublime level of purity. (R. Chaim Vital, cited in *Or Hachamah* on *Zohar* II:10a. See also the extensive discussions in *Moreh Nevuchim* II:28-29; *Teshuvot Harashba* I:9; and *Shenei Luchot Haberit, Bet David*.)

10. See above, sect. 24.

11. I.e., "he shall not leave his holy status" (*Sanhedrin* 19a).

12. *Cf.* above, sect. 76.

blessed be He,[13] and immediately restore your thought to the original attachment. David thus said to his son Solomon: "I am going the way of all the earth," (I Kings 2:2) i.e., like a person on a journey with his mind and desire set to return home with the greatest haste.[14]

---

13. When your thought is focused on the Supernal World, you never leave it; for, as stated above, sect. 69, you are where your thought is.
14. "The righteous . . . consider this world insignificant, and their dwelling here is but temporary . . . Even as a stranger yearns to return to his birthplace, they, too, long to return to their root and origin." (R. Bachya, *Kad Hakemach, s.v. ger*)

85

Do not say, "I will pray on *Shabbat* with *kavanah* (concentration), but not on weekdays."[1] For you are not to be like servants of the king who apply themselves to their work in the presence of the king but will not do it conscientiously in his absence. A person like that is not a faithful servant.[2]

You must realize, with [proper] faith, that without the King it is bad for you. Thus repel all the guards until you come before the King. [3]

You may not be able to speak before [the King], nor be worthy to come into His presence. Nonetheless, He will grant you your wish, for He is exceedingly merciful to you.

---

1. *Shabbat* is an especially auspicious holy day. The "other side" (impurity) is set aside, and there is a manifestation of radiant Godliness. The prayers of the *Shabbat* are especially beloved on high. (See *Zohar* II:135aff. and III:243a). "The gate of the inner court . . . shall be shut during the six working days, but on the *Shabbat* it shall be opened." (Ezekiel 46:1; see *Zohar* I:75b). On weekdays, therefore, prayer needs much more effort.
2. Moreover, to think that you will pray with *kavanah* on *Shabbat* after neglecting this duty all week long, will simply not work, as explained below, sect. 131.
3. This refers to the parable cited above, sect. 72, and below, sect. 86.

86

Do not say: "I will pray when I am able to do so with *hitlahavut* (ardor; fervor); but otherwise I will not force myself to pray." On the contrary! It is comparable to a king who changes his garments when waging battle. Those who are familiar with the king recognize him by his mannerisms. Those who are not familiar with the king note that people guard a certain place more [than others]; thus it may be assumed that the king must be there. So, too, if you are unable to pray, it means that the King is guarded from being manifest to you. Thus strengthen yourself so much more, for the King is here but He is hidden from you.[1]

---

1. This section basically repeats the theme of sect. 72; see there.

87

Bear in mind that in prayer you proceed from chamber to chamber. When an alien thought comes [to your mind] you are expelled, because you are judged in every chamber whether you are worthy to enter.[1]

Thus if you are not praying with *hitlahavut* (ardor; fervor),[2] start to pray intensely. When you pray with *hitlahavut*, consider the nature of the [alien] thought:[3] if it relates to evil love, such

---

1. This paragraph is based on *Zohar* II:245b. See also below, sect. 89.
2. An alien thought may be cast into your mind by Divine Providence, which of itself means expulsion from the chamber, as you lacked *kavanah* or did not pray with *hitlahavut* (see the Baal Shem Tov's teaching in *Maggid Devarav Leya'akov*, sect. 84, and *Keter Shem Tov*, sect. 287). Thus it should bestir you to strengthen yourself, to pray intensely (*cf.* above, sect. 58, 72 and 86).
3. The alien thought may be cast into your mind in context of "a descent for the sake of an ascent" (see above, sect. 64, and the notes there) in order that you sublimate that thought (see *Keter Shem Tov*, sect. 207). This is, though, a hazardous task which requires a degree of spiritual perfection (see above,

as sensuous lust, bring it to its [ultimate] source which is the love of God.[4]

There are only seven types of thought. They correspond to the "seven days of creation."[5] Each [of these] has an *erev* (evening) and a *boker* (morning).[6] *Erev* is an expression of *ta'aruvot* (mixture), i.e., having an alien thought; and *boker* is an expression of *bikur* (visit), i.e., visiting God.[7] The [seven types of thought] are then "love of God" and "love of sin;" "fear of God" and "bad fear" such as hatred; "[good] glorification" of glorifying God and "bad [glorification]" of self-glorification; and likewise with *nitzu'ach* (endurance; victory), *hodayah* (acknowledgment; thanksgiving; praise), *yessodot* (foundations)

---

sect. 13-14, note 3). Thus you can undertake this task only when you pray with *hitlahavut*.

4. See above, sect. 22. The sequel of this section (as also below, sect. 90, 101, 120 and 127) explains the sublimation of all possible categories of alien thoughts.

5. The "seven days of creation" signify the lower seven *Sefirot*, i.e., the *midot* (attributes) of *Chessed, Gevurah, Tiferet, Netzach, Hod, Yessod* and *Malchut*. Just as these attributes are to be found in the realm of Divinity and holiness, so, too, they are to be found in the realm of impurity and evil (see above, sect. 13, note 2). Everything in creation contains sparks of the *Sefirot*, either of the *Sefirot* of holiness or of the *Sefirot* of impurity. In man, the *midot* are reflected in corresponding soul-faculties, in two parallel categories: the seven emotive attributes of man's Divine soul relate strictly to holiness (*Chessed*—love of God; *Gevurah*—fear or awe of God; and so forth); and the seven emotive attributes of man's animal soul which relate to his physical reality and pursuits, thus to the realm of that which is not holy or even evil (*Chessed*—love of material objects or sin; *Gevurah*—fear of material objects, or its consequences like anger; and so forth).

6. The numbering of the days of creation (Genesis 1) is introduced with the phrase "It was evening and it was morning."

7. *Cf. Bereishit Rabba* 3:8: "'It was evening' refers to the deeds of the wicked; 'it was morning' refers to the deeds of the righteous."

i.e., the sense of bonding.[8] Each of these [seven] is compounded of ten [aspects].[9] With every bad thought one gives vitality, Heaven forbid, to the "seven nations."[10]

Midrash Hane'elam (*Zohar* I:86b) thus states: [When God created] the world, it was wavering to and fro. The Holy One, blessed is He, then said that Abraham—i.e., the attribute of love[11]—will come forth into the world. But there will also be the issue of Ishmael, i.e., [the attribute of] "bad love."[12] A thought of "bad love," therefore, gives vitality to Ishmael and the nine [aspects] that go with him. There is also Isaac, i.e., the attribute of "[good] fear;" and [correspondingly] Esau [the attribute of] "bad fear," i.e., murder. A thought of "bad fear,"

---

8. See above, note 5. The attribute of *yessod* signifies bonding, joining together. The author does not mention here the attribute of *malchut* (kingship; sovereignty). It would relate to accepting the sovereignty of God on the good side, and submission to evil or impurity on the bad side.

9. There are altogether ten *Sefirot*: the upper three (*Keter, Chochmah* and *Binah*; or, on the immanent level, *Chochmah, Binah* and *Da'at*), and the seven *midot*. Each of these subdivides into ten levels of inter-relationships with the other *Sefirot*. *Chessed* thus compounds *Chochmah* of *Chessed*, *Binah* of *Chessed*, *Da'at* of *Chessed*, *Chessed* of *Chessed*, and so forth; and likewise with all the others. (*Tikunei Zohar* 47:84a and 69:116b)

10. Evil thoughts, and sins in general, are not just failures on the part of man. They have a cosmic effect of strengthening (infusing vitality into) the seven attributes of the realm of *kelipah* (see also below, sect. 90). The "seven nations" of the early inhabitants of the Holy Land signify these seven attributes of the realm of impurity (see above, sect. 13-14, note 2).

11. The Patriarchs signify the first three attributes of holiness (Abraham—*Chessed*; Isaac—*Gevurah*; Jacob—*Tiferet*), and later saints (Moses, Aaron, Joseph and David) the other four respectively (*Zohar* III:301b-302a). See below, sect. 139.

12. Ishmael and Esau are the dross of Abraham and Isaac respectively (*Sifre, Ha'azinu*, par. 212, and *Berachah*, par. 343; *Pesikta Rabaty*, ch. 39; *Tikunei Zohar* 15:30b). Ishmael thus signifies *chessed* of *kelipah* and Esau *gevurah* of *kelipah* (see *Zohar* III:124a and 246b).

therefore, gives vitality to Esau and the nine [aspects] that go with him, Heaven forbid.

Thus if you happen to think of a "bad love,"[13] say to yourself: "What have I done? I have taken a part of the World of Thought[14] and brought it to a place of filth!" This will effect that you be subdued and come to the [level] of dust, thus bringing the thought to the attribute of *ayin* (naught).[15] Then you will come to the World of Love by reminding yourself: "If I love this object, as, for example, a woman, who is but a 'putrid drop,'[16] how much more should I love God!"[17]

Likewise, when you hear words of jest which cause you to be mirthful, think that it is but a part of the World of Love. Also, when you see or eat something that gives you pleasure, think that it is but a part of the World of Delight. Thus take heed not to crudify that delight, and "then you will find pleasure *al* (lit.: over) God" (Isaiah 58:14), i.e., *beyond* [the level of the Divine] Name [*Havayah*; the Tetragrammaton], as it were.[18] Your whole being, therefore, should be directed to that

---

13. Negative *chessed*.

14. Vitality from the realm of thought that originates in holiness; for thought is made up of letters which in their origin are sparks of the *Shechinah* (see *Maggid Devarav Leya'akov*, sect. 47).

15. The realization of wrong-doing leads to subduing and negating the ego ("I am as dust and ashes"—Genesis 18:27), the level of *ayin* (naught; self-negation). In the supernal realm of *ayin* all breaches can be corrected, and all sparks ascend to holiness (see *Maggid Devarav Leya'akov*, sect. 98 and 232).

16. *Avot* 3:1

17. In other words, you forsake the incidental and insignificant and pursue the primary and essential. See above, sect. 84, and below, sect. 90.

18. See *Zohar* II:83a: "It does not say '*im* (with) *Havayah*,' but '*al* (over) *Havayah*'.. i.e., the place from whence those above and below derive, and they desire that place, of which it is written '[I raise my eyes over the mountains] *me'ayin* (from whence; but in Kabbalistic terminology taken literally: 'from *ayin*—naught', which is a term for the highest *sefirah* of *Keter*, the ultimate sphere of the World of Delight) will come my help' (Psalms 121:1), and it is

pleasure in context of it being part of the World of Delight. Thus you may sit and eat here, yet be in the World of Delight. The pleasure that you caused yourself, therefore, will bring delight unto God in all worlds.

Likewise, when you see something of which you are afraid,[19] say to yourself: "Why should I be afraid of this? It is but a human like myself—let alone if it is but an animal or beast! As the awesome God, blessed be He, is vested in that being [enabling it to exist], how much more should I fear [God] Himself!"[20]

The same applies to glorification.[21] When people praise you, or you sense pride in the midst of prayer, or people exalt you for your concentrated study, bring yourself to a sense of awe—i.e., shame—before God.

---

written 'and reached unto *Atik Yomaya* (the Ancient of Days; in Kabbalistic terminology generally signifying the realm of *Keter*) and they brought him near before Him' (Daniel 7:13). The longing and delight of the righteous is to contemplate that splendor, for every [form of] splendor is emitted from there and from it emanate all those crowns (i.e., *Sefirot*)."

The Tetragrammaton signifies *Ze'eir Anpin*, the compound of the *midot* from *Chessed* to *Yessod*. To ascend "above *Havayah*," therefore, is to ascend beyond the *midot* to their very source.

19. Negative *gevurah*.

20. This does not mean that one is to ignore danger, for it is Halachically forbidden to expose oneself to danger and to rely on miracles (*Pesachim* 64b; *Ta'anit* 20b; *Zohar* 111b; Maimonides, *Hilchot Rotze'ach Ushmirat Hanefesh* 11:4ff.; *Shulchan Aruch, Yoreh De'ah* 116:5). Thus one must avoid danger and make every effort to escape it. The Baal Shem Tov deals with sublimation: when something mundane arouses fear in man, he should utilize that opportunity to consider the ultimate source of fear and generate within himself the fear of God. One is to consider that the present—*unintended*—confrontation of danger is by Divine Providence (*cf.* below, sect. 120), thus think of God, even while using the *Divinely* endowed gift of intelligence to observe the *Divine* precept to save himself.

21. The attribute of *Tiferet*.

In context of *nitzu'ach*,[22] overcome that trait or have your understanding lead you to a sense of "Divine victory." Do the same with the aspect of *hodayah*;[23] and also with "bonding,"[24] i.e., to be bound up with God alone.

---

22. The attribute of *Netzach*.
23. The attribute of *Hod*.
24. The attribute of *Yessod*.

88

You should show compassion for the *Shechinah* when speaking in a way that removes the words from God.[1] Normally you ought to be overcome by fear when speaking, because the "World of Speech" is the "World of Fear."[2] Thus, indeed, when speaking with a sense of love and awe [of God], you will be overcome by fear, and when continuing that way you will reach a level of immense *hitlahavut* (ardor; fervor).

---

1. See above, sect. 75, note 10. The Baal Shem Tov taught: The *Shechinah* is in exile because all words of speech derive from Her and ought to be for the service of the Creator but, by our many sins, these words are used for material matters, idle talk and falsehoods. (*Darkei Tzedek* I:20) See also *Maggid Devarav Leya'akov*, Addenda, sect. 33.

2. The *Shechinah* is the World of Speech (above, sect. 75, note 7), the *Sefirah* of *Malchut* (ibid., note 11). The attribute of fear relates to *Gevurah* (above, sect. 87), but it is rooted in *Binah*, the "supernal *Shechinah*" (see sect. 75, note 11). Thus it is reflected in the "lower *Shechinah*," in *Malchut* (which, therefore, is called the "lower *Gevurah*"; *Zohar* III: 269b): "'Fear of God' is the *Shechinah*, the holy *Malchut*" (*Tikunei Zohar* 33:77a; also *ibid.* 7b). Realizing the identity of *Shechinah* and speech, and minding this when speaking, therefore, will generate a sense of fear:

   "When thinking before prayer about what you will say, and before whom you are speaking, fear and shame will surely come upon you. When considering that the World of Speech, i.e., the *Shechinah*, speaks through you, you will be afraid of the words themselves . . . How can you not be overcome by fear and shame when you know that you bestir the *Shechinah*." (*Maggid Devarav Leya'akov*, sect. 78; cited in *Keter Shem Tov*, sect. 313.)

89

When beset by an alien thought, feel extremely ashamed because you have been expelled from the King's palace.[1] Return to the palace with great embarrassment and exceeding humility. To harbor an alien thought is a [grave] sin tantamount to begetting a *mamzer*,[2] as it is said (*Ketuvot* 103a) "ewe follows ewe, [as the mother so is her daughter]."[3]

Thought has a male and a female aspect. So, too, sound and speech correspond to male and female.[4] The utterance of words of holiness while harboring an alien thought is like a *mamzer* whose external form is as that of a *kosher* (fit; legitimate) person but the inner reality is evil. [In our context,] the words spoken are letters of holiness, but the thought [behind them] is evil. For with holy speech [joined to] thoughts of something else you beget a *mamzer*.

Bear in mind also, that as your thought is wandering among other matters, the Holy One, blessed is He, says: "Why did you come into the *teivah* (word) when I am not in it?!"[5]

---

1. See above, sect. 87.
2. A *mamzer* is the offspring of a union between a man and woman whose marriage would be a capital offense or incur the Heavenly penalty of *karet* ("excision," which implies premature death), such as incest and adultery. In our context, *cf. Massechet Kallah* ch. 1 (and see also *Nedarim* 20b) that some are regarded like *mamzerim* though legally they are not. One of these is *mamzer temurah*, i.e., one begotten with the alien thought of someone external.
3. I.e., the offspring reflects its origin. The status of the *mamzer* reflects the transgression of his parents. So, too, the alien thought reflects its origin in the illegitimate union of holiness and evil, as explained in the next paragraph.
4. See *Zohar* III:228a-b. *Cf. Likkutim Yekarim*, sect. 131.
5. It would seem preferable to emend this sentence as in the version of *Maggid Devarav Leya'akov*, sect. 148: "The Holy One, blessed is He, says: 'Why is it that I came and there is no man' (Isaiah 50:2) in the word." That is, man's thought, which is the very soul of his speech, was not in the word.

90

"You fill their belly with *tzefuncha* (that which is hidden with you) . . . [they leave their *yeter* (abundance; remainder) to their babes.]" (Psalms 17:14)

Avoid gazing at material things that are attractive. How much more so, avoid gazing at the beauty of women to indulge your desire. For that type of looking is self-worship, which is like worshipping idolatry.[1] [Moreover,] that thought leads, Heaven forbid, to nocturnal sin.[2] Thus you will add strength to *kelipah* ("husk;" the forces or realm of evil), impregnating it.[3]

This is the meaning of *tzefuncha*, i.e., that which you *tzofeh* (observe) for your sake, such as the beauty of a woman. By looking for self-indulgence you add power to [*kelipah*].

Moreover, if you do so before giving birth to a child, your child will be rooted in the power [of the *kelipot*].[4] R. Isaac Luria, of blessed memory, thus explained [the ruling] that "Honor your father." (Exodus 20:12) includes [the obligation to honor] your elder brother (*Ketuvot* 103a): The older brother is like the major branch of a tree. As another branch grows from that major branch, it draws vitality from the major branch. So, too, the younger brother draws vitality from the older one.[5] Thus it follows that when first infusing strength

---

1. "Whoever gazes at the beauty of a woman by day will have [lustful] thoughts at night, and if he brings that thought upon himself he will violate the prohibition of 'do not make for yourself molten gods' (Leviticus 19:4)." (*Zohar* III:84a; *cf.* R. Bachya on Leviticus 19:2).

2. *Avodah Zara* 20a-b. *Cf. Nedarim* 20a; and above, note 1.

3. See above, sect. 87 (and note 10 there).

4. The quote cited above, note 1, continues that the children one begets under the influence of those thoughts "are called 'molten gods;' that is why it is written, 'Do not turn to the idols and do not make for yourselves molten gods.'"

5. R. Chaim Vital, *Likkutei Torah, Vayeira; Sha'ar Hamitzvot, Yitro*.

into *kelipah* and then begetting a child, that child will be like the smaller branch. The principal strength is [given] into [the forces of evil], and the child is like *yitron*, something additional. This is the meaning of "they left their *yitron* to their babes."

Thus when seeing things, conduct yourself as follows:

If you suddenly happen to see a beautiful woman,[6] think to yourself: "Whence is her beauty? If she were dead she would no longer look this way; thus where does her [beauty] come from? Per force it must be said to come from the Divine force diffused within her.[7] It gives her the quality of beauty and redness. The root of beauty, therefore, is in the Divine force. Why, then, should I be drawn after a mere part! I am better off in attaching myself to 'the root and core of all worlds'[8] where all forms of beauty are to be found."[9]

It is likewise when observing other physical objects, such as a vessel. Think to yourself: "Whence came beauty and form to this vessel? Its material substance is clearly worthless. Its beauty and form, however, are the spiritual and vital reality of the vessel, which is a Divine portion from Above [for the vitality of all physical things is a Divine portion from Above].[10]

Likewise when eating, bear in mind that the taste and sweetness of the food derives from the vitalizing force and sweetness of Above, and that is its vitality. For inorganic matter, too, has a vital force as evident from the fact that it has

---

6. That is, beyond your control.
7. See *Nidah* 31a: a person's beauty comes from God.
8. *Zohar* I:11b
9. This principle is stated already above, sect. 87. See also below, sect. 120 and 127.
10. The vital force of everything is a spark of the *Shechinah*. See next note, and below, sect. 109.

existence and durability.[11] It follows, then, that the Divine vitality from Above is to be found everywhere.

When viewing things this way, you are looking at them with your mind, and it is not done for self-indulgence but related to the *En Sof*, blessed is He. This is effective for negating [improper] thought.

It is an established principle that what you think during the day affects the thoughts you have when sleeping and dreaming.[12] Thus by following the above procedure all day long, you will merit to see in your dreams the vital force of that physical object. Your sight (empirical perception) during the day is but of the physical; but when your thought dwells on the spiritual reality vested in the physical, then in your dream you will see the bare spirituality divested from its [external] garment.[13] For [the term] *chalom* (dream) is an expression of "periods of *chalim*" (*Rosh Hashanah* 28a), which means strong, sound.

In daytime man's vital force is weak because he is bound up with his [physical] body; that is why he does not see the vital force inherent in physical matters. At night, however, the vital force extends beyond the body; thus it is strong and allows one to perceive the vital force itself. This may bring one to levels of prophecy.[14] Thus it is written of all prophets that "I speak to him in a dream" (Numbers 12:6), except for Moses,

---

11. "Even inorganic matter—i.e., dust, stones and so forth—of necessity possesses a spiritual life-force," as do also all vegetation, animals and humans. (R. Chaim Vital, *Eitz Chayim* 39:3. See *Tanya, Sha'ar Hayichud*, ch. 1-2.)

12. See *Berachot* 55b; *Zohar* I:183a.

13. See *Or Hachamah* on *Zohar* 183a.

14. "Dream is a sixtieth part of prophecy;" *Berachot* 57b. See *Zohar* I:147a; and *Moreh Nevuchim* II:36. *Cf.* Maimonides, *Hilchot Yessodei Hatorah* 7:1.

our teacher, peace be upon him, who was able to perceive the vital force of physical matter even when awake.[15]

[King] David thus said: "*Echezeh* (I will see) Your face in righteousness, [I will be sated with Your image when awake]." (Psalms, *ibid.* verse 16) *Echezeh* is an expression of "*chizayon laylah*" (a vision at night; Job 33:15), [thus implying a vision of] "Your face" itself at night. Why [did he merit this]? Because "I will be sated with Your image when awake." "Image" alludes to the form.[16] Thus, "when noting something physical, I will not look just at its matter but will also consider that its image—i.e., its form and vital force—are 'from You,' and He is vested in that matter."

This is the meaning of "The wise one's eyes are in his (alternatively: its) *rosh* (head)" (Ecclesiastes 2:14), that is, in the "head" of the object, its spirituality and vital force.[17] This is also the meaning of "The *rosh* (head; beginning) of Your word is truth" (Psalms 119:160), and of "You are exalted as *rosh* (head) over all" (I Chronicles 29:11), in context of the *Zohar's* concept of "*Reisha dechol reishin*—the Head of all heads."[18]

---

15. See *Hilchot Yessodei Hatorah* 7:2 and 6.

16. *Moreh Nevuchim* I:3

17. The wise one's mind is focused on the *rosh*—the "head" or true reality, i.e., the spirituality and vital force—of everything, as opposed to the external appearance. (See above, sect. 73, note 3, that *rosh* refers to the *Shechinah*, the Divine Immanence.)

18. *Zohar* III:10b, 11a and 289b (and in several places in *Tikunei Zohar*). It signifies the supreme *Sefirah* of *Keter*, from whence derive all other "heads" (i.e., the Divine emanations that constitute the essence, the spirituality and vital force, of everything).

91

Sometimes you must exhibit pride towards others for the glory of the Creator,[1] as our sages said (*Sotah* 5a) that a Torah-scholar ought to have "one eighth of an eight's [of pride]."[2] However, be very careful to consider at the time your own baseness, saying to yourself: "In truth I am very base, and my proud demeanor is but for the glory of the Creator, blessed be He. For myself I do not need any pride, for 'I am a worm and not a man' (Psalms 22:7); thus why would I want honor?"[3]

1. Pride, arrogance, is a cardinal sin in religious ethics in general, and in Chassidism in particular (see below, sect. 102). Nonetheless, there is a "good pride," of which it is said "his heart was elevated (proud) in the ways of God." (II Chronicles 16:6) That pride is not detrimental to the ideal of humility, but aids and increases it (*Chovot Halevovot, Sha'ar Hakeniyah*, ch. 9; and see there also ch. 6, rule 6). It is pride in God and Torah, thus leads to service of God and the performance of *mitzvot*, even as negative humility is repellent to these (see *Keter Shem Tov*, sect. 68 and 393).

2. A Torah-scholar represents the honor of Torah. For himself he must be humble, like everyone else. At the same time, however, he must also remember what he represents and conduct himself accordingly (see Maimonides, *Hilchot De'ot*, ch. 5; and *cf. Hilchot Talmud Torah* 6:10 and 12). In that context he must exhibit (*externally—cf.* Maimonides, *Hilchot De'ot* 1:4-5 and 2:3) a minimal sense of pride, i.e., "one eight of an eight's." (For a definition of this amount see Maimonides' commentary on *Avot* 4:4, and for a mystical definition see R. Tzvi Hirsh Kaidanover, *Kav Hayashar*, ch. 65. This symbolic amount is chosen because it represents the content of the smallest instrument for measuring in Halachah (*Tossafot, Rosh Hashanah* 13a, *s.v. chassar*).)

3. *Cf.* above, sect. 12, 42-43,, 48, 55, 57; and below, sect. 114, 122, 124 and 131.

92

Pride, even the slightest thought of it, is a very grave matter.[1] Any ulterior motive derives from pride. Every thought is a

1. Generally one should choose a middle path (the "golden mean"). As for pride and anger, however, one must remove oneself to the furthest extreme

complete structure.[2] [With pride, therefore,] one causes a serious blemish Above and "repels the feet of the *Shechinah*," as it is written "Every one who is proud in heart is an abomination to God." (Proverbs 16:5)[3]

---

away from them. These two traits are tantamount to idolatry (*Hilchot De'ot* 2:3; and *cf.* above, sect. 49). The positive pride discussed in the preceding section does not contradict this principle: it is not personalized, that is, it is not a mater of self-esteem, but exclusively for the glory of God. In that sense, then, the Baal Shem Tov teaches that "Pride purifies the defiled, and defiles the pure": A false sense of humility, thinking to yourself "I am not fit to approach God," defiles, because it prevents you from pursuing your obligations. It is overcome (you are purified) by the pride of "his heart was proud in the ways of God" (see above, sect. 91, note 1). On the other hand, the seemingly pure who fulfills his obligations is defiled by his pride, by the self-satisfaction and self-esteem in his service of God. (*Keter Shem Tov*, sect. 393)

2. "Every letter is a complete world" (below, sect. 118), containing "worlds, souls and Divinity" (above, sect. 75); and "every word is a complete structure" (above, sect. 34). This applies to thought as well, for thought is composed of letters and words (see above, sect. 87, note 14). As a complete or self-contained structure, therefore, it affects the totality of reality, including the spiritual realms.

3. "The Holy One, blessed is He, declares of anyone with arrogance, 'I and he cannot both dwell in the world;' as it is said. 'I can not bear him who is with haughty eyes and proud heart' (Psalms 101:5)." (*Sotah* 5a)

The Baal Shem Tov taught that this passage proves that pride is worse than blatant sin: Of all forms of sin and impurity it is said "Who dwells with them amid their impurity" (Leviticus 16:16; i.e., the *Shechinah* remains among them despite their spiritual contamination; *Yoma* 56bf.). Of the proud and arrogant, however, it is said, "I and he cannot both dwell in the world." (Cited by R. Ya'akov Yossef of Polnoy, *Tzafnat Pane'ach, Yitro,* p. 76d).

93

When speaking to people, first attach yourself mentally to the Creator, blessed be He. The soul of the other, too, is

[then] bound up with the Creator. For every person lives but by virtue of the [Divine] emanation infused into all creatures.[1]

Bear in mind that your words are but spoken before the Creator, blessed be He, to bring gratification unto Him; thus "I am not speaking to my fellow, for what difference does his praise or reproach make to me [i.e., whether he will praise or reproach me."[2] All this is from the Baal Shem Tov, may the memory of the righteous be for blessing, for the life of the world to come.]

---

1. Speech is rooted in the *Shechinah*, the "World of Speech" (see above, sect. 75, note 7). As sparks of the *Shechinah*, therefore, the words of speech reflect the vitality of man (see below, sect. 103). Moreover, "good speech" ascends on high, bestirs the "supernal speech" (i.e.. the *Shechinah*) and effects the emanation of additional vitality (*ibid.*). By addressing your words to others, with prior attachment of your thought (the soul of speech) to on high, the Divine vitality of these words is infused in the listeners, and their souls, too, become bound to the Creator. *Cf. Keter Shem Tov*, sect. 113 and 251, where this principle is applied in particular to the context of rebuking others: the speaker's prior attachment to on high, to the common root of all souls, establishes a relationship with the listener.

2. Your words are attached to Above, and become a channel for Divine emanation, only when spoken for the sake of Heaven, without ulterior motives (such as self-glorification). Thinking of yourself while speaking will disrupt the bond and the flow of vitality. See below, sect. 103.

94

"In all your ways *da'eihu* (acknowledge—*lit.*: know—Him)." (Proverbs 3:6) This is an important principle: *Da'eihu* is an expression of "joining together,"[1] i.e., joining the *hei* to the *vav*,[2] in all your dealings, even in your physical involve-

---

1. The root-word of *da'eihu* is *yada* (to know), which signifies attachment and union (as in Genesis 4:1; *Tikunei Zohar* 69:99a). See below, sect. 99.

2. *Da'eihu* can be divided into two parts: *da* (know; in our context: join together), and *hei-vav* (the last two letters of the word). The letter *hei*, as last

ments.[3]

---

letter of the Tetragrammaton, signifies the *Sefirah* of *Malchut*, the *Shechinah* (the ultimate life-force that enables man to act). The *vav*, as second-last letter of the Tetragrammaton, signifies the *Sefirah* of *Tiferet*, or the compound of the six *Sefirot Chessed* to *Yessod* (in Kabbalistic terminology referred to as *Ze'eir Anpin*—'Minor Visage'), represented by the term the "Holy One, blessed is He." *Da'eihu* thus means to effect the "unity of the Holy One, blessed is He, and His *Shechinah*" (see above, sect. 43, notes 7-8).

3. The beginning of our proof-text ("In all your ways") signifies all your dealings, all your physical or mundane engagements (*Hilchot De'ot* 3:3; *Shulchan Aruch, Orach Chayim*, 231). Thus: "In all your ways" join the act (signified by the *hei*) to the *vav*. The physical or mundane engagement itself will thus be sublimated to holiness and spirituality.

     This is then clearly a great (all-comprehensive) principle, as already stated in the Talmud: "What short text is there upon which all the essential principles of the Torah depend? 'In all your ways acknowledge Him.'" (*Berachot* 63a)

     Note above, sect. 81, for advice how to go about in attaining this goal.

95

[Another important principle:] Your service must be but for the sake of Above, without any other intent.[1] Not even the slightest intent should be for your own sake, but [altogether] for the sake of Heaven.[2]

---

1. This section essentially repeats the theme of the preceding one. There, however, the focus is on the sublimation of the physical. Here the emphasis is on preserving the purity of the Divine service: your prayer, your study of Torah, your *mitzvot*, must all be for the sake of God, without any ulterior motives that involve the ego, even if it be for spiritual attainments.

2. See also above, sect. 3, 11, 73 and 84; and below, sect. 122-123; on the principle of *avodah tzorech gevohah* (service for the sake of Above).

96

Citing R. Israel Baal Shem:

"Beware of their *gachelet* (glowing coal) lest you be burnt ...
all their words are like fiery *gachalot* (coals)." (*Avot* 2:10) This is
difficult to understand: if the unqualified term *gachelet* implies
burning [coals; embers], why then qualify it [in the conclusion as] "*fiery* coals"? If again, *gachelet* is defined to relate to
omemot, i.e., *dimmed* (dying coals), why would you need to be
careful "lest you be burnt" as *gachelet* simply refers to *omemot*?

[The Baal Shem Tov], of blessed memory, thus said:

A perfect *tzadik* (saint) may sometimes fall from his level
and worship God in a mode of *katnut* (constricted consciousness):[1] he does not pray with great *kavanah* (intention), and
sometimes may even go idle.[2] Another person seeing the *tzadik*
in that state of not praying or studying with great *kavanah*, and
sometimes going idle, may very well think to himself that he
can act likewise. After all, if the saintly and pious can do so,
how much more so he himself! The teacher [of our *Mishnah*]
thus cautions: "Do not compare yourself to the Torah-scholar
and *tzadik*! For when the *tzadik* will awaken from his 'sleep'[3]
and again prays and studies as he used to, he will elevate all his
idle words [or deeds].[4] You, who observed him, however, you
are but a simple person who is totally unaware of the mystery

---

1. See above, sect. 67 and 69 on the concept of *katnut*.
2. I.e., externally he is not engaged in the service of God.
3. His temporary descent to *katnut*.
4. *Cf. Zohar* II:245b: "The improper prayer is expelled, descends and hovers in
    the lowest firmament . . . remaining there until that person will do *teshuvah*..
    If he returns properly to his Master and offers another prayer properly, as
    that good prayer ascends—the overseeing [angel] makes the improper
    prayer arise to meet up with the good prayer: thus they become intermin-
    gled, ascend together and enter before the Holy King." In other words, that
    which was originally deficient can subsequently be rectified and elevated by
    proper intent.

of Divine worship. How dare you, then, compare yourself to him!"

This is the meaning of "beware of their glowing coals":

Even when [*tzadikim*] have fallen from their level and are like "dimmed coals" for uttering idle words or involved with idle deeds, beware! Do not apply a lesson from them [for yourself], for even their idle talk is like fiery coals, as stated above.[5]

---

5. The *tzadik* is always attached to Godliness. To him applies, even in his state of *katnut*, "I concealed (treasured) Your word in my heart so that I will not sin against You" (Psalms 119:11). (*Keter Shem Tov*, sect. 77 and 366) He retains the ember, fiery coals, even when that fire is dimmed and not apparent. His burning sparks can restore the great flame (see above, sect. 67, note 3) that will sublimate everything of his temporary fall. This cannot be said, however, of one who is not a *tzadik*: if he engages in idle talk or deeds, he may not only be unable to sublimate these, but remain on their level (see *Keter Shem Tov*, sect. 356; and *cf.* also *Maggid Devarav Leya'akov*, sect. 65, and *Likkutim Yekarim*, sect. 113).

97

"If I am not for myself, who is for me? [But when I am for myself, what am I?]" (*Avot* 1:14)

When you pray, you must be divested of physical reality. This is the meaning of "If I am not for myself"—i.e., when I am thus divested—then "who is for me?," i.e., I am not afraid of alien thoughts. "But when I am for myself, what am I?," i.e., in my state of self-awareness there are many alien thoughts.[1]

The saying "When I am here, all is here" (*Sukah* 53a), too, can be interpreted in like manner.[2]

---

1. Up to here is a brief version of sect. 62; see there.
2. Offhand the implication is as follows: "If I am here, everyone is here; but if I am not here, who is here?" Thus: "If I"—ego and self-awareness—"am

here, everyone"—i.e., the alien thoughts—"is here;" but "if I am not here"—i.e., if I am divested of ego and physical awareness, the state of self-negation, then "who is here"—i.e., alien thoughts will not approach me. Note, though, the interpretation in *Or Torah*, sect. 431, which is followed by the text of our sect. 97 as a sequel.

98

"Every prudent man acts with *da'at* (knowledge; fore-thought), [but the fool *yiphros* (spreads out) [his] folly." (Proverbs 13:16) This means that the wise man does every-thing with *da'at*,[1] even his [personal] transactions.[2] The fool,[3] however, even when succeeding in becoming a communal leader or head,[4] it is but folly.

1. With attachment (*deveikut*) to Godliness; see above, sect. 94, note 1 (and below, sect. 99).
2. The principle of "Acknowledge Him in all your ways." See above, sect. 94.
3. He who acts without *deveikut*.
4. This seems to be an extended interpretation of *yiphros* as a *notarikon* (an acrostic abbreviation) for *parnes-rosh* (leader-head). The more elaborate ver-sion of this teaching in *Maggid Devarav Leya'akov*, sect. 237, however, renders the more likely (and simpler) interpretation of reading *yiphros* as "becoming *parush*—abstemious (from worldly involvements)," as the root-words of both are essentially the same. The reading there is: "he is *parush* from the world and continuously studies Torah; but he studies and prays without *deveikut* to the Creator, blessed be He, doing so only for self-esteem and to be called rabbi. [Thus for him] 'it is folly.'"

99

"The *tzadik* (righteous; saint) *yode'a* (knows) the *nefesh* (desire; lit. soul) of his animal." (Proverbs 12:10) This means that he joins even that *nefesh*[1] to the service of the Creator.[2] For the word *yode'a* is an expression of "joining together."[3]

---

1. I.e., the *nefesh* of his animal soul, his involvements with the physical and mundane. (See R. Meir ibn Aldabi, *Shevilei Emunah*, VI; cited in *Shenei Luchot Haberit*, *Sukah*, p. 77b.)
2. A variation on the theme stated above, sect. 94 and 98.
3. See above, sect. 94, note 1.

100

Citing R. Israel Baal Shem:

"*Yisas'char chamor garem*—Issachar is a large-boned donkey." (Genesis 49:14) This verse indicates that "*yesh-sachar* (there is reward; earning)[1] that *garam* (is caused)[2] by *chomer* (physical matter)."[3]

---

1. The name *Yisas'char* can be divided into the two words "*Yesh sachar*—there is a reward (or earning)." *Zohar* I:158a.
2. By a slight change of vocalization, *garem* is read *garam*. This interpretation appears already in *Nidah* 31a and *Zohar* I:157b (with an explanation in *Bereishit Rabba* 99:10.)
3. *Chamor* is read as *chomer*. This is a a frequent reading in mystical writings (see R. Judah Loewe, *Gevurot Hashem*, ch. 29; and *cf. Torah Shelemah* on Exodus 4:20, note 109).

    This is again a variation on the theme of sect. 94, 98 and 99. Sublimation of physical matter and reality causes great gain and reward, i.e., great spiritual effects. *Cf. Keter Shem Tov*, Addenda, sect. 91.

101

In the name of the Rabbi, the Preacher of the Holy Community of Mezhirech[1]

[a] In the act of coition you must regard yourself as naught.[2] This is the meaning of "Rabba drove away the flies" (*Nidah* 17a), i.e., he did not consider himself even as a fly.

---

1. R. Dov Ber of Mezhirech, disciple and successor of the Baal Shem Tov.

[b] [³ Regard yourself as no more than a tool. When a craftsman hits the rock with a hammer, this happens because of *his* desire, and not because of the hammer's desire, to hit the rock; for if it had been the latter, (the hammer) would be independent of the craftsman. Thus things happen according to the infusion of the primordial mind into the tools.

All of (man's) limbs are but tools: he needs to eat but cannot do so without his tools. He is not to eat to indulge his desire, as he is not to love anything but God and His commandments. Cohabitation is necessary to preserve the species (lit.: the generation), for this cannot be except by the cohabitation of male and female. As he and she are but tools, however, one should not cohabit to indulge desire, and one is not to love anything but God and His commandments. Thus—]

love your wife just like your *tefillin* (phylacteries) which you care for only for the sake of observing the command of God.⁴ Do not muse on her.⁵ Regard it like someone traveling

---

2. "'Sanctify yourselves and be holy' (Leviticus 11:44); this teaches that a person must sanctify himself during cohabitation." (*Zohar Chadash, Bereishit* 11a) The principle of self-negation ("regard yourself as naught") and acting for the sake of Heaven (see above, sect. 94-95 and 98-100) applies here no less than with any other physical engagements (see Maimonides, *Hilchot De'ot* 3:2 and 5:4-5; *Shulchan Aruch, Orach Chayim*:231, and *Even Ha'ezer*:25). The mystical writings are very emphatic on the sanctification of this act (see especially *Zohar* I:112a and III:80a and 81b; *Zohar Chadash, Bereishit* 11a-b; *Reishit Chochmah, Sha'ar Hakedushah*, ch. 16).

3. The preamble, i.e., the bracketed passage, does not appear in *Tzava'at Harivash* but in the version of *Or Ha'emet*, p. 7b, and *Likkutei Amarim* (manuscript of R. Menachem Mendel of Vitebsk), p. 40a.

4. This does not mean to exclude the basic or ideal sense of love. After all, "the sages ordained that a man is to honor his wife more than his own self and love her as himself" (*Yevamot* 62b; Maimonides, *Hilchot Ishut* 15:19). It excludes an objectified love of the wife that is contingent on self-serving consideration, such as self-gratification (*cf. Avot* 5:16). The sensual aspect of

to a market, and he cannot do so without a horse. Would he, therefore, come to love the horse?[6] Is there anything more foolish than that? Likewise, in this world a man needs a wife for the service of the Creator[7] in order to merit the World-to-Come.[8] Could anything be more foolish than to forsake his affairs[9] to muse on her? Rather, spurn her [being a sexual object].

When you see a beautiful woman[10] think to yourself that the white substance is from the seed of the father and the red substance is from the seed of the mother,[11] turbid blood, putrid and repugnant, which placed next to food would render that food loathsome. The beauty sown by the [physical] father derives from the Supernal Father,[12] the "World of Love,"[13] while the seed of the mother derives from the Supernal Mother,[14] the "World of Fear."[15] This is the beauty [of the

---

cohabitation is only a necessary means towards a higher end. In that context, the husband and wife are but "tools" to achieve that end, just as *tefillin* are the "tools" to fulfill the command of God. (Note that *Zohar* III:81a-b draws an analogy between *tefillin* and the union of husband and wife.)

5. Do not keep thinking of her in context of self-gratification.

6. I.e., he would not be obsessed about the horse which is merely his "tool" for transportation.

7. The personal benefits from the spouse are but incidental to the spiritual benefits effected by marriage, i.e., for the service of God.

8. See *Yevamot* 62b*ff.*

9. Man's principal affairs to serve God and fulfill his function on earth.

10. This paragraph deals with the sublimation of thought. This subject has already been dealt with, in detail, above, sect. 87 and 90, as well as sect. 14 and 22.

11. *Nidah* 31a

12. The *Sefirah* of *Chochmah* (*Zohar* III:290a*ff.*).

13. Love is identified with the *Sefirah* of *Chessed* (*Tikunei Zohar* 6a and 10b); but *Chessed* is rooted in *Chochmah*, the "Supernal Father" (*Zohar* II:175b and III:118b). Thus *Chochmah* is the ultimate "World of Love."

14. The *Sefirah* of *Binah* (*Zohar* III:290a*ff.*).

woman]. Thus it is better to attach yourself to the love and fear of the Creator, blessed is He.

By rendering that sin[16] repugnant in your eyes, all sins will be repugnant in your eyes. For it accounts for the formation of man,[17] who has 365 sinews alluding to the 365 prohibitions [in the Torah].[18] [Spurning lust, therefore,] negates [the violation of] the 365 prohibitions.[19]

R. Israel Baal Shem, peace be upon him, thus said: There is a great desire for this sin[20] because it accounts for the formation of man.[21] Man most likely derives pleasure from his eating and other things, [for] all forms of pleasure derive from that [seminal] drop. Thus he is attached with everything to *katnut* (constricted consciousness).[22] It is far better to attach himself to the Holy One, blessed is He.[23]

---

15. Fear is identified with the *Sefirah* of *Gevurah* (*Tikunei Zohar* 10b); but *Gevurah* is rooted in *Binah*, the "Supernal Mother" (*Zohar* II:175b and III:118b). Thus *Binah* is the ultimate "World of Fear." *Cf.* above, sect. 88.
16. The sin of indulging sensual self-gratification.
17. The pursuit of pleasure leads to cohabitation, which, in turn, brings about the formation of man. See below, note 21.
18. *Zohar* I:170b
19. The control and sublimation of the ultimate root of all violations enables man to avoid these.
20. See note 16.
21. "Were it not for the evil desire, no man would build a house, take a wife and beget children." (*Bereishit Rabba* 9:7; and see *Zohar* I:61a.)
22. To be in the grips of physical pleasure means attachment to the physical. The consciousness of the Divine, therefore, is (at least) weakened and restricted.
23. By analyzing the pleasures, as stated above, and sublimating them to their spiritual sources.

102

"*Havayah* (GOD) shall be for me *Elokim* (God)." (Genesis 28:21)[1] That is, [you are to] "Acknowledge Him in all your ways" (Proverbs 3:6), whether it is something good or bad.[2] Thus if, Heaven forbid, something bad happens to you, consider that it is surely to atone your sin.[3] On the other hand, the *tzadik* should worry about good things happening to him, because they may be at the expense of his merits.[4] This is the meaning of "*Havayah* shall be for me *Elokim*": *Havayah*, [signifying] the attribute of mercy, may in fact be [for me] the attribute of judgment indicated by [the Name] *Elokim*;[5] thus I must continuously increase [my] merits.[6]

1. God is referred to by a variety of names, each signifying one of the Divine attributes. The Tetragrammaton (conventionally rendered *Havayah* to avoid pronouncing this ineffable name), signifies the Divine attribute of mercy, compassion. *Elokim* signifies the attribute of Divine judgment. (*Sifre* on Deuteronomy 3:24; *Zohar* III:65a)
2. I.e., acknowledge the presence and workings of God in everything that happens to you, whether it be perceived as good or bad. *Cf. Berachot* 54a: "Man must bless God for bad things just as he blesses Him for good things."
3. See *Berachot* 5a.
4. The *tzadik* does not take it for granted that he deserves the Divine benevolence. He assumes that when good things come his way, he is using up the merits he has accumulated. See *Shabbat* 32a; *Tanchuma, Lech*:10; and Rashi on Genesis 32:11.
5. The Almighty does not withhold the merited rewards of any creature (*Baba Kamma* 38b). The *tzadik*, however, is to worry that the good things happening to him imply compensation in this world for his merits. This would be a negative sign of Divine judgment, because "the righteous are rewarded in the world to come . . . the wicked are rewarded in this world" (*Ta'anit* 11a).
6. *Cf.* the interpretation of our proof-text in *Zohar* I:151a: "Even the mercy I shall regard to myself as judgment, so that I will serve [God] continuously."

103

Speech is the vitality of the human, and that vitality comes from [God], blessed be He.[1] Thus when a person utters "good speech," that speech ascends on high and stirs the Supernal "Speech." This, in turn, effects that further vitality emanates to him from on high.[2].

If, however, a person speaks something that is bad, the vital force has departed from him and will not ascend. Thus it is likely that his total vitality may cease from him altogether. This is indicated by the vernacular expression "*er hot oysgeredt*—he has spoken [it] out."[3]

1. "When a person speaks, breath comes out of his mouth. That breath is part of his vitality . . . it derives from his soul . . . That is why why we are enjoined not to engage in idle talk because it causes one to lose part of his soul." (R. Chaim Vital, *Likkutei Torah*, *Ekev*, on Deuteronomy 8:1-3) See also above, 75, note 7; and sect. 88 and 93, and the notes there.
2. The word coming from the mouth of man ascends and bestirs an arousal from Above, for good or for bad (*Zohar* II:47b). When man emits a holy word from his mouth, a word of Torah, it produces a sound that ascends on high and bestirs the holinesses (i.e., the *Sefirot*) of the Supernal King and they crown his head, and there is joy above and below (*ibid.* III:105a).

   "When [people] speak good [words] and attach thought to that speech, they join the World of Speech to the World of Thought and effect good. Likewise, when they speak bad [words], they effect evil, Heaven forbid;" *Keter Shem Tov*, sect. 273 (and see my notes there).
3. I.e., he has exhausted the vitality.

104

Sometimes one is to serve God just with the soul, i.e., in thought, keeping the body static so that it will not become ill from using it extensively.[1]

1. See above, sect. 59, and below, sect. 105. *Cf.* also above, sect. 58, notes 5-6.

105

Sometimes one can recite the prayers with love and fear, and great *hitlahavut* (fervor; burning enthusiasm), without moving at all, so that to another it may appear that he is saying the words without any *deveikut* (attachment to God).[1] [When strongly attached to God] one can serve Him with the soul [alone], with immense and great love [of God].[2] This is the best kind of worship. It proceeds faster, with greater *deveikut* to God, than prayer that is externally visible in the limbs.[3] *Kelipah* ("husk"; force of evil) cannot attach itself to this [ideal] prayer, because it is altogether inward.

---

1. See above, sect. 58-59, 65, 68 and 104.
2. See above, sect. 65 and 68.
3. See *Keter Shem Tov*, sect. 226.

106

Citing R. Israel Baal Shem:

When the body ails, the soul, too, is weakened,[1] and one is unable to pray properly[2] even when clear of sins. Thus you must guard the health of your body very carefully.[3] Up to here [is this quote].

---

1. *Cf.* the admonition of the Maggid of Mezhirech: "A small hole in the body causes a big hole in the soul." (*Maggid Devarav Leya'akov*, Addenda, sect. 191)
2. Physical infirmity (including the weakness incurred by fasting) undermines the powers of the mental faculties, "for it is impossible to understand the subjects of wisdom and to meditate upon them when he is ill or one of his limbs is aching" (Maimonides, *Hilchot De'ot* 3:3 and 4:1).
3. *Hilchot De'ot* 3:3 and 4:1; and *cf. Moreh Nevuchim* 3:27, that the welfare of the soul can only be achieved after obtaining the welfare of the body.

107

Prayer with great joy[1] is certainly much more acceptable before [God], blessed be He, than prayer in sadness and with weeping.[2]

A parable for this would be the case of a pauper petitioning and beseeching a king with great weeping: he will receive but

---

1. "One is not to pray in a state of sadness but with joy" (*Berachot* 31a). "The root of prayer is the heart's rejoicing in God" (*Sefer Chassidim*, sect. 18).

2. See above, sect. 44-45. "'Rejoice before Him' (Psalms 68:4), for 'before Him' there is no sadness at all, for ['before Him'] all is joy (Chagigah 5a) . . . . Thus it is written 'Serve God with joy' (Psalms 100:2), for one is not to show sadness [in His service] . . . What about one who is troubled and in distress, thus unable to rejoice in his heart, and because of his distress seeks compassion from the Supernal King? Is he to refrain from prayer altogether to avoid entering with any sadness? Surely, however, it was taught (*Baba Metzi'a* 59a) that all gates have been closed, but the gates of tears have not been closed. Tears are caused by sorrow and sadness. Thus those appointed over the gates break down all detours and locks and take in those tears. That prayer will then enter before the Holy King." (*Zohar* II:165a) Likewise, weeping is appropriate in prayers related to *teshuvah*—e.g., confession of sin and asking for forgiveness (see above, sect. 45, note 2), or the prayers of the midnight-vigil (see above, sect. 16, note 1). All other prayers, however, and the service of God in general, must be with joy. R. Isaac Luria thus rules:

   "It is prohibited to pray before God in a state of sadness. [One is to pray] but like a servant attending to his master with great joy, for otherwise the soul does not have the capacity to receive the supernal illumination that is drawn into him by means of his prayer. Sadness is appropriate only with the recital of confession and when remembering one's sins. With all other prayers, however, *one is not to consider any sadness—not even concern about sins one has committed.* To be sure, it is good that one be humble when praying, but with great joy. This is a very important matter, and it is proper to be careful with it. This matter is beyond estimation [of its value]." (*Peri Eitz Chayim, Sha'ar Olam Ha'assiyah*, end of ch. 1 (in ed. Koretz, *Sha'ar Hakorbanot*, ch. 2); *Naggid Umetzaveh, s.v. Bet Haknesset*, p. 40)

   The act of prayer implies faith and trust in God which, in turn, imply (and of themselves must lead to) joy and gladness of the heart (see *Reishit Chochmah, Sha'ar Ho'ahavah*, ch. 12).

little. With a minister, however, who joyfully recounts the king's praises before him and in that context also submits his request, the king will give him a very large gift as befits the minister's stature.[3]

---

3. "The world below is always in a state of receiving . . . and the upper world gives to it in accordance to its condition: if it is with radiating countenance, they will be radiant to it in kind from on high. If it is in a state of sadness, it is given judgment in kind.. Thus it is written 'Serve God with joy,' for the joy of man draws forth another joy, the supernal one." (*Zohar* II:184a, and see there also end of 218a.)

108

When praying, have in mind that God is vested in the letters.[1] This means:

We do not know what a person thinks unless he speaks. It follows, then, that speech is a garment for thought.[2] Say, then, to yourself: "I am preparing a garment for such a great King; thus it is only proper that I do so joyfully."[3] Utter the words, therefore, with all your strength,[4] because that will effect unity with [God],[5] blessed be He. As your strength is in the letter[s], and the Holy One, blessed be He, dwells in the letter[s], you are united, therefore, with [God], blessed be He.[6]

---

1. See above, sect. 75, 88 and 103.
2. The thought is vested in speech.
3. *Cf.* above, sect. 107.
4. See above, sect. 34, 58 and 75.
5. I.e., closeness and attachment to God.
6. See above, sect. 75.

109

"The Torah is concerned about the money of Israel." (*Yoma* 39a) Why so?

It is an important principle that when you wear, eat, or make use of anything, you derive benefit from the vital force inherent in that object.[1] The object could not exist without that spiritual component, and it contains holy "sparks" (nitzotzot)[2] that relate to the very root of your soul. I heard that this is the reason why a particular thing is loved by some people and disliked by others who love something else.[3]

When using some thing or eating food, therefore, even if you did so for your bodily needs,[4] you rectify those "sparks." They are rectified by virtue of you using the strength added to your body by the garment, food or other things, to serve God. Thus it may happen that when you complete the rectification of all those "sparks" in that object which relate to the root of your soul, God takes it away from you and gives it to someone else because its remaining "sparks" relate to that other person.[5]

R. Israel Baal Shem, peace be upon him, thus said: [when] people eat and sit with others and use others, it means that they are dealing with the "sparks" in those things. A person, therefore, must be concerned about his objects and everything

---

1. See above, sect. 90, and notes 9-10 there. The pervasive principle that everything contains holy sparks which man must redeem and restore to their source, is explained at length in R. Chaim Vital, *Likkutei Torah, Eikev,* and idem, *Sha'ar Hamitzvot, Eikev.*

2. See below, sect. 141.

3. I.e., the natural or innate likes and dislikes of a person relating to certain edibles, garments or utensils.

4. Provided that you do so in legitimate manner (e.g., kosher food) and, as explained further on, the energy or benefit generated by them is used for good purposes.

5. When something comes your way it is by Divine Providence and grace. You are given the opportunity to fulfill your mission on earth to redeem the sparks that are meant to be elevated by you. On the other hand, sometimes a person is deprived of that opportunity, as a punishment, as explained above, sect. 31.

he has, because of the "sparks" they contain, i.e., to show concern for the holy "sparks."[6]

---

6. This concern parallels the concept of concern or compassion for the *Shechinah*, explained above, sect. 88.—On the themes of this section see also *Keter Shem Tov*, sect. 194.

110

You are to serve God with [both] fear and joy. These are "two friends that do not separate [from each other]."[1] Fear without joy is melancholy.[2] It is inappropriate to feel anguished in considering how to serve God,[3] but always be joyful. For even then you must still serve [God],[4] and there is no spare time to consider how and what.

---

1. Fear and joy related to one thing are two contrary feelings. In the service of God, however, they do not contradict one another but can go together hand in hand (see *Yalkut Shimoni*, Psalms, sect. 623; *Zohar* III:56a). This coexistence is unique. It is possible only in the service of God (*Keter Shem Tov*, sect. 349; *cf. Sifre* on Deuteronomy 6:5). See also below, sect. 128, on compounding love and fear in the service of God.
2. "Fear of God" is one of the 613 precepts of the Torah (Deuteronomy 6:13). It is a prerequisite to the service of God, "the foundation of all wisdom and the 'gate to God'" (see above, sect. 66, and also sect. 15). Nonetheless, it must coexist simultaneously with joy ("Serve God in joy;" see above, sect. 107), which is the unavoidable effect of true faith and trust in God. For fear on its own leads to gloom and dejection. By the same token, joy on its own leads to carelessness and frivolity (see below, sect. 128).
3. I.e., the anguish from worrying whether you are doing the right thing, or doing so sufficiently. This worry leads to a sense of worthlessness and dejection. See above, sect. 44 and 46; and *cf.* also end of sect. 2-3.
4. I.e., your prime concern at all times must be to act and serve God, and to do so with joy. See above, sect. 44 (especially note 3) and 46.

111

". . . and to become attached unto Him." (Deuteronomy 11:22) How can you attach yourself to [God] when He is a "devouring fire" (Deuteronomy 4:24)? It means, "attach yourself to His attributes: as He is merciful, so you be merciful."[1] That is:

Worship of God with *hitlahavut* (fervor; burning enthusiasm) implies total *deveikut* (attachment) to [God], blessed be He. It is, though, impossible to be in that state continuously, for it is but "reaching and not reaching" (*Zohar* I:16b),[2] like fire: by blowing at fire at the beginning [of kindling it] you extinguish it; but when doing so later on, the flame increases and the fire itself comes down, thus ascending and descending, [always] moving. So, too, it is with *hitlahavut*: it is "reaching and not reaching;" for "continuous pleasure is no pleasure."[3]

The *Gemara* thus queries: "After all, He is 'a devouring fire'?" This relates to *hitlahavut* which ceases from you , it is "reaching and not reaching." How, then, is it possible to become attached to Him, blessed be He? The answer is: "attach yourself to His *midot* (attributes), i.e., to His "garments," to the "letters."[4] It is possible to continuously keep thinking of the letters of the Torah, and the Torah is His "garment," blessed be He. Thus even when speaking to people, think but of the

---

1. This paragraph is a compound of two statements in *Sifre* on Deuteronomy 11:22, which appear also as separate statements in the Talmud—*Ketuvot* 111b, and *Shabbat* 133b (also *Sotah* 14a).

2. I.e., as you reach the supernal level you must withdraw, because it is impossible to endure the intensity of the supernal light (see *Maggid Devarav Leya'akov*, sect. 166, 201 and 225). It is analogous to the concept of "*ratzo veshov*—running and returning," discussed above, sect. 67, note 1.

3. This is an oft-cited aphorism of the Baal Shem Tov. *Cf. Moreh Nevuchim* 3:24.

4. See above, sect. 108.

[letters] of the words, for they, too, are from the twenty-two letters of the Torah.[5]

---

5. All words are rooted in the 22 letters of the alphabet, whether the speech relates to matters of holiness or to the mundane (see *Keter Shem Tov*, sect. 373). These letters originate in, and contain, Divinity (see above, sect. 75). Thus when considering the Divine source of speech, you retain a degree of *deveikut* even in the state of "not reaching," when the *hitlahavut* has ceased. (Note, though, that mundane speech involves the danger of being led astray by it. Thus one must pray for Divine assistance to retain the proper perspective. See below, sect. 140.)

112

"As He is *rachum* (merciful), [so you be merciful]." (*Shabbat* 133b)

[The word] *rachum* has the same letters as *chomer* (matter). The implication is as follows: It cannot be that the Holy One, blessed is He, should show mercy to turbid matter, for how can the thoughts of the Most Refined encompass turbid mater? He can show mercy to us only when constricting Himself, blessed be He, so that His thought may encompass matter.[1] How does such *tzimtzum* (constriction) come about? When man is merciful, he effects that the Holy One, blessed is He, vests Himself in His "garment" and, as it were, constricts Himself, and also shows mercy unto him.[2] This is the meaning of "As He is merciful . . ," and this is how one effects mercy.

---

1. The concept of *tzimtzum*; see above, sect. 84, note 6.
2. The principle of reciprocity of God relating to man "measure for measure." See above, sect. 31, note 3; 107, note 3; and below, sect. 142.

113

Torah-study must be forceful and with great joy. This will diminish alien thought[s].[1]

---

1. This is a duplication of sect. 51

114

"Better is he who is lightly esteemed and a servant [to himself] than one who is honored but lacks bread." (Proverbs 12:9)

The sole sign for the [true] service of the Creator is when you know of yourself that you are lightly esteemed in your own eyes.[1] For then you are on a [spiritual] level, thus "a servant unto Him," blessed be He. [That is better than] "the one who is honored" in his own eyes, [for the latter] "lacks bread," i.e., [the Divine] effulgence.[2]

---

1. *Cf.* above, sect. 53.
2. This interpretation of the term "bread" appears in R. Mosheh Cordovero, *Pardess Rimonim* 23:11, *s.v. lechem.*

115

A parable from ice: If there is thick ice which later becomes thin, the rivers may overcome the ice and flow over it, but [the ice] remains firm. If, however, we see that the ice is thin, and not firm,[1] it follows that the ice was not strong to begin with.

Likewise, when we see that one serves [God] some times but not at others, it is certain that he has not yet served prop-

---

1. I.e., after the waters of the river passed over it.

erly. For if he had served once properly, he would be doing so continuously.[2]

2. I.e., once you have tasted the beauty and delight of the proper service ("Taste and see that God is good;" Psalms 34:9), you will pursue it continuously. In context of the parable: "Many waters (of the mundane entanglements) cannot extinguish the love, and rivers cannot wash it away." (Song 8:7)

116

"Righteousness will go before him and will set his footsteps on the path." (Psalms 85:14) In terms of ethical admonition, this means the following:

Some people set out to perform a *mitzvah*, like praying and so forth, but stop midway to speak to others. Though he will yet perform the *mitzvah* thereafter, it is accounted to him as a sin for not having done so with alacrity. His punishment after death will be "measure for measure": various texts state that [after death] one is made to cross a river by a very narrow ford. This causes him very great suffering, because he is filled with fear and trembling. Yet he must run very fast, because speedy crossing is of the essence. Now in the midst of the way and crossing, the Holy One, blessed is He, sends an angel to hinder him. This angel is the one created by that *mitzvah* [mentioned above].[1] The angel, however, had been subjected to suffering. For the thought (resolve) at home to go and perform the *mitzvah*, creates the soul of the angel, and its body is created by the act of the *mitzvah*.[2] Thus just as the creation of his body was delayed by the person stopping to speak with

1. Every meritorious act creates a "good angel," and every sin creates a "bad angel." See above, sect. 17, note 2.
2. Thought, *kavanah* (intent), is the soul to its effects in speech or action. (R. Chaim Vital, *Eitz Chayim* 40:3; and see *Keter Shem Tov*, sect. 284.) See above, sect. 58, note 4; and below, sect. 126.

others, this angel now, too, came to hinder him in the midst of his crossing so that he will be unable to run.

This, then, is the meaning of "Righteousness goes before him," in the plain sense. For all *Mitzvot* go before a person after his death.[3] When going to perform a *mitzvah*, therefore, one must see to do so with alacrity, and not with laziness.[4] Thus "it will set his footsteps on the path," and he will not be hindered when crossing the river.

---

3. Every *mitzvah* or meritorious deed one performs in this world precedes him and walks before him in the world to come, as it is said, "your righteousness shall go before you" (Isaiah 58:8). (*Avodah Zara* 5a; *Pirkei deR. Eliezer*, ch. 34.)
4. See above, sect. 20.

117

"The words of his mouth are evil and deceit; he has ceased to be wise, to do good." (Psalms 36:4) That is, because of "The words of his mouth," i.e., of the *yetzer hara*, "he has ceased to be wise, to do good."[1] This means:

The *yetzer hara* will surely not entice you not to study Torah at all. He knows that you would not listen to that.[2] For if you do not study at all, people will not esteem you and you will not be called a scholar.[3]

---

1. This section is a variation (with different wording but essentially the same idea) on the interpretation of our proof-text above, sect. 74; see there.
2. "Such are the wiles of the *yetzer hara*: to-day he says to [man] 'Do this,' to-morrow he tells him 'Do that,' until he will say to him 'Go and serve idols;' and he goes and serves [them]." (*Shabbat* 105b) In other words, the *yetzer hara* achieves his end by gradual enticement which is not recognized by the victim as going astray.
3. These are ulterior motives that one is not to have when studying Torah (see *Nedarim* 62b). This initial sin provides the *yetzer hara* with an opening to entangle man further, as stated above, note 2.

The *yetzer hara* thus entices you not to study whatever would bring you to fear of Heaven,[4] such as works of *mussar* (devotional subjects),[5] or *Shulchan Aruch* (the code of Jewish law) from which you would know the law properly.[6] He entices you to study constantly nothing but the Talmud with all the commentaries.[7]

---

4. Thus making you ignore the admonition that Torah-study is to be the gate leading to the court of fear of Heaven (*Shabbat* 31b), to *teshuvah* and good deeds (*Berachot* 17a).

5. See above, sect. 1, on the Baal Shem Tov's insistence on daily study of such works.

6. See *Keter Shem Tov*, sect. 423, on the Baal Shem Tov's insistence on study of *Shulchan Aruch*.

7. This is not a critique of traditional Talmud-study, but only of the kind that is not *lishmah* (for its own sake as a Divine precept) and divorced from the religious goal of *deveikut*, attachment to God (*cf.* above, sect. 29 and 54, and below, sect. 119). Talmud-study and *pilpul* (dialectic discussions of Talmudic subjects) that is *lishmah* is "*kishutei kalah*—the bridal adornments" of the *Shechinah* (*Zohar Chadash, Shir*:64a), causing delight unto God even when one arrives at mistaken conclusions (*Or Torah*, sect. 397; *Maggid Devarav Leya'akov*, sect. 88). Thus "one must be very careful not to neglect Torah-study. One is to be as studious as possible and observe 'this book of the Torah shall not depart from your mouth' (Joshua 1:8).. Study *Torah-Nevi'im-Ketuvim* (the Books of the Bible) every day until becoming familiar with them. Study *Mishnah* every day, to correct what one has blemished. Study *Gemara* (Talmud) with *iyun* (intensive, deliberate study), for the study of *Gemara* with *iyun* breaks asunder the *kelipot*; but it must be *lishmah*." (*Likkutei Amarim*—teachings and instructions of the Maggid of Mezhirech—from the manuscript of R. Menachem Mendel of Vitebsk, p. 26a; *ibid.*, ms. of R. Shemuel Shmelka of Nikolsburg, II:ch. 1 (published in *Torat Hamaggid*, p. 1). The last three sentences—[which appear also in nearly identical wording (with additional requirements) in the *Hanhagot Yesharot* of the Maggid's senior disciple, R. Menachem Nachum of Czernobyl, preceding his *Me'or Einayim*, Brooklyn NY 1975]—are based on the principles stated in R. Chaim Vital, *Peri Eitz Chayim, Sha'ar Hanhagat Halimud*; and see also *idem, Sha'ar Hamitzvot, Va'etchanan. Cf.* also *Darkei Tzedek* V: p. 18a, quoting the Maggid, that intensive Talmud-study to the point of discovering new insights (*chidushei Torah*) purifies man's thought for the service of God.)

This, then, is the meaning of "he ceases," i.e., the *yetzer hara* seeks to make man cease "to be wise, to do good." He prevents man from occupying himself also with that kind of study that will have a good effect upon him, i.e., fear of Heaven.

The parallel-version of our section in *Likkutim Yekarim*, sect. 237, renders: "nothing but *pilpulim* (dialectic discussions of Talmudic subjects) that are *inauthentic*, as explained in the sacred *Shenei Luchot Haberit*" (see there *Massechet Shevu'ot*, p. 30d). This critique of the sophistry of "inauthentic *pilpul*" is not unique to Chassidism. It appears not only in the much earlier *Shenei Luchot Haberit* but was voiced already earlier by R. Judah Loewe of Prague (see his *Tiferet Yisrael*, ch. 56; *Netivot Olam, Netiv Hatorah*, ch. 5; *Derech Chayim*, ch. 6), and other Rabbinic authorities that preceded Chassidism.

118

When meditating in prayer on all the *kavanot* (mystical devotions) known to you, you are but meditating on those you know. On the other hand, when you say the word with great *hitkashrut* (bonding), all *kavanot* are included in the whole word of themselves and by themselves. For every letter is a complete world. Thus when you say the word with great *hitkashrut*, surely you bestir those supernal worlds and thereby achieve great effects.

You must, therefore, see to pray with great *hitkashrut* and *hitlahavut* (fervor; burning enthusiasm); for surely you then bring about great effects in the supernal worlds, because every letter causes a stirring Above.[1]

---

1. On the contents of this section see above, sect. 34, 75 and 108, and the notes there.

119

When studying Torah have in mind the saying in the *Gemara* (*Berachot* 8a)[1] that "The Holy One, blessed is He, has nothing in the world but the four cubits of *Halachah*." Say to yourself that He, blessed be He, constricted Himself and dwells here; thus it is appropriate to study with joy, fear and love.[2]

---

1. *Cf.* above, sect. 54.
2. See above, sect. 108, which *mutatis mutandis* relates no less to the letters of the Torah. See also above, sect. 51.

120

I heard from R. Israel Baal Shem, peace be upon him:

Why is it called "World of Freedom"? Because even a slave entering there becomes a free man.[1] This means:

As known, every thing came about by the emanation from the Holy One, blessed is He, through His attributes of love and fear. The love, however, is in exile, vested in the material, as in women or food.[2] When man considers that this love is a "garment" unto [God], blessed be He, and, Heaven forbid, he

---

1. "You shall sanctify the fiftieth year and proclaim freedom throughout the land for all its inhabitants; it shall be *yovel* (a Jubilee Year) for you . . . each of you (i.e., all slaves) shall return to his family." (Leviticus 25:10) In the Kabbalistic scheme of the *Sefirot, yovel* signifies *Binah: Binah* is the World of Freedom (see *Zohar* I:124b and II:183a). In context of the exposition following, "all slaves" refers to the "enslaved" sparks of holiness in everything, which, when raised to *Binah* (the Supernal *Shechinah*) are freed: in *Binah* they are corrected and freed (see *Maggid Devarav Leya'akov*, sect. 78).
2. The two Divine attributes of love and fear are reflected in their mundane counterparts, i.e., in the love and fear man has towards objects in physical reality (see above, sect. 90, and the notes there).

has divested Him, blessed be He, from His garment,[3] he ought to tremble with great anxiety as he remembers his evil deeds. He ought to feel ashamed and disgraced, and say to himself: "If I love this which is but a love that fell with the 'breaking [of the vessels]'[4] and is vested in a 'putrid drop,'[5] how much more should I love Him, blessed be He!"[6]

The same applies to fear. When afraid of a heathen—or of [a weapon like] a sword—he should say to himself: "Why should I be afraid of a human like myself? Surely the Creator, blessed be He, is vested in that human; thus how much more should I be afraid of Him, blessed be He!"[7]

It is likewise with glorification, and all the other [attributes].

Also, when you hear someone speaking while you pray, say: "Why did God bring him here to speak while I pray? All this must be by *hashgachah peratit* (Divine Providence relating to all particulars). Speech is identified with the *Shechinah*.[8] The *Shechinah* thus is vested in the mouth of that person in order that I strengthen myself for the service [of God].[9] How much, then, must I strengthen myself in the 'service, i.e., prayer' es-

3. I.e., by using his attributes of love and fear (which ultimately originate in the Divine) for the physical and mundane, he "exiles," as it were, the sparks of Divinity they contain.
4. The Kabbalistic metaphor of "*shevirat hakeilim*—the breaking of the vessels" of the Divine attributes in the process of creation, which accounts for the diffusion of holy sparks throughout creation.
5. I.e., in man (see *Avot* 3:1).
6. See above, sect. 87 and 90, and below, sect. 127.
7. See above, sect. 87, note 20.
8. See above, sect. 75, note 7, and 88.
9. I.e., the unavoidable disturbance is itself by Divine Providence in order that I overcome it; "a descent for the sake of an ascent" (see above, sect. 64).

pecially if that man speaking is a gentile or a minor."[10] It follows, then, that the *Shechinah* is, as it were, in that person; thus it is but appropriate for you to act with alacrity.

---

10. This reference to a gentile aroused the ire of the opponents to Chassidism. They regarded it blasphemous to suggest that when a gentile's speech disrupts prayer, this is possible only because the *Shechinah* is vested in his mouth. Ostensibly they were disturbed by the original text of *Tzava'at Harivash* which states "the *Shechinah dwells* in the mouth of that person." Rabbi Schneur Zalman of Liadi was confronted with that complaint and wrote a lengthy reply demonstrating the orthodoxy of this principle. He concedes that the term "dwells" is inappropriate, blaming it on the incorrect translation into Hebrew of the Baal Shem Tov's Yiddish (the language in which he taught), and should be emended to "is vested in." (He adds, however, that this does not appear to be the opponents' major objection: it seems that they question the basic principle of the *Shechinah* being vested in *every thing*, including the *kelipot*, notwithstanding the fact that this is stated clearly in the Kabbalah in general, and in the teachings of R. Isaac Luria in particular.) The reply appears in *Tanya, Igeret Hakodesh*, sect. 25.

There is a significant difference between the expressions of "dwells in" and "is vested in." *Hashra'ah*, "indwelling of the *Shechinah*," implies a *revelation* of Divinity. The object of the indwelling merges into the light of God and its reality is completely dissolved in Him. This relates strictly to the realm of holiness. The light of God does not abide nor manifest itself in any thing whose reality is not completely nullified in Him. *Halbashah*, "investment of the *Shechinah*," implies no more than a flow of light and vitality from the *Shechinah* by way of *tzimtuzm*, i.e., by occultation and concealment of the original light and vitality: it is an exceedingly minute portion of light and vitality, just sufficient to supply the recipient with the necessary "life-force" that allows the recipient to exist *ex nihilo* and to be in a state of finitude and limitation. No thing can exist without this investment of vitality, whether it be human, animal, vegetable or inorganic matter (though, obviously, the amount or degree of the concealed light differs from one object to another). See *Tanya*, ch. 35 and 48; and *cf. ibid., Igeret Hakodesh*, sect. 23.

121

"There are four principal categories of damage: the *shor* (ox); the *bor* (pit); the *mav'eh* (consumption); and the fire." (*Baba Kama* 2a)[1]

Shor (ox) is an expression of "*ashurenu*—I shall look at him" (Numbers 23:9 and 24:17), i.e., an expression of looking and gazing. It refers to the [kind of] sight that is harmful to people.[2]

Bor (pit) is an expression of "*s'dei boor*—an empty (fallow) field, that is not ploughed and sown."(*Baba Metzi'a* 104a) It refers to one who does not study but walks around idle.[3]

Mav'eh denotes "Tooth." It refers to one who eats every thing.[4]

"Fire" refers to anger, conflagration.[5]

---

1. These legal categories of damage relate to torts on the physical level. Here we are taught how they relate no less to the spiritual level. This is done by implicit extension of the terms, or by reading them as idioms of similar root-words (a common device in Midrashic and Chassidic writings, as, e.g., above, sect. 1, 2, 16, 71, 90; below, sect. 122, 124 and 138).
2. See above, sect. 5 and 50, and the notes there.
3. See above, sect. 29, and the notes there.
4. On the physical level of torts this relates to one's animals consuming another's foodstuffs. On the spiritual level it refers to indulging the animal soul's desires for food and drink. This self-indulgence desensitizes man's spiritual nature and leads astray (*Sifre*, and Rashi, on Deuteronomy 11:15; *Berachot* 32b). See below, sect. 131.
5. On the physical level of torts this relates to one person's kindling of fire causing damage to another. On the spiritual level it refers to the cardinal sin of anger, rage (see above, sect. 92, note 1).

122

"Rabbi said: Which is the right way that a man *yavor* (should choose) for himself? [Whatever is glorifying to the doer himself and brings him glorification from man. And be as careful with a 'minor' *mitzvah* as with a 'major' one, for you do not know the reward given for *Mitzvot*.]" (*Avot* 2:1) This means:

"Which is the right way" refers to "which character-traits must be avoided?" For [the word] *yavor* is an expression of [*boor*,] "emptiness."[1]

Thus he continues, "Whatever is glorifying for the doer himself . . ." The implication is to perform a *mitzvah* in secret, with no one knowing about it.[2]

If, however, you think to yourself that you serve God, [and this leads you] to a sense of self-glorification, let alone [when anticipating that] "it brings him glorification from man," i.e., doing the *mitzvah* in order to be praised by others—that they shall say that your are a God-fearing person, you must refrain from all [such thoughts].[3]

If you act in this manner, you will be "as careful with a 'minor' *mitzvah* as with a 'major' one," for then "you do not know the reward given for the *Mitzvot*."[4] You will act solely to bring gratification to the Creator, blessed be He, without [an-

---

1. See above, sect. 121, note 1. The sentence thus reads: "Which is the right way of what man is to empty (clear) himself of?"

2. I.e., the "right way" is to act without any ulterior motives. In our context, he has "emptied" himself of self-glorification (self-satisfaction) and the desire to be glorified by others. Thus he acts in secret, relating strictly to God, as the opinions of others do not matter to him. *Cf.* above, sect. 65, and also sect. 11, 15, 55, 87 and 114.

3. I.e., he must refrain from all such thoughts ("that a man should clear himself of"). It does not mean to refrain from performing his religious duties, even if it be not yet in the "right way." See above, sect. 55 and 64, and below, sect. 126.

4. I.e., the Mishnah is not to be read as two separate admonitions. The phrase "and be as careful . . ." is taken to mean "and then you will be as careful . . ." So, too, the phrase "for you do not know . . ." is taken to mean "*because* (i.e., for the very reason that) you do not know (i.e., that you do not pay attention to) the reward."

ticipation of] any compensation of reward that may cause self-glorification.

On the other hand, pursuit of self-glorification, will cause you to consider whether a *mitzvah* is [merely] 'minor'; for [only] a 'major' *mitzvah* will bring you glory, thus you will not observe the 'minor' one.[5]

---

5. This is obviously unacceptable. There are legal differences between a "major" *mitzvah* and a "minor" one, but both are equally commands of God with all that this implies. See above, sect. 1 and 17.

123

"Three books are opened on Rosh Hashanah: [one for the thoroughly wicked, one for the *tzadikim gemurim* (perfectly righteous), and one for the *beinunim* (intermediate)...]." (*Rosh Hashanah* 16b)

Tzadikim gemurim are those whose speech is altogether in matters of holiness, prayer and Torah, to unite the speech with the "World of Thought."[1] For one must believe that with every prayer and word of Torah, when uttered with *kavanah* (proper intent), you surely unify the "World of Speech" with the "World of Thought."[2] You may not be granted that which

---

1. The "World of Speech" (*Malchut*; the "lower *Shechinah*") is reflected in human speech. The "World of Thought" (*Binah*; the "supernal *Shechinah*") is reflected in human thought. Man must effect the *yichud* (unification) of these two by infusing his proper speech (words of prayer and Torah) with proper thought (*kavanah*). See above, sect. 75, especially notes 11-12. Those whose sole intent is to effect that supernal *yichud* are the perfectly righteous.

2. Note *Maggid Devarav Leya'akov*, sect. 53: You must consider that you are but like a tool. Your thought and speech are extensions of the [supernal] worlds (see above, note 1). Thus the "World of Speech" (i.e., the *Shechinah*) beseeches the "World of Thought" for the spiritual aspects of the prayer's content. As the "World of Thought" (*Binah*; the supernal *Shechinah*) extends the requested effusions to the "World of Speech" (*Malchut*; the lower *Shechinah*), this effects also the literal fulfillment of the prayer on the mundane

you requested in your prayer.[3] Nonetheless, the "stirring from below," unifying the "World of Speech" with the "World of Thought," effects the same on high.[4] These people, therefore, whose sole intent is to unify the "World of Speech" with the "World of Thought," they are *tzadikim gemurim*.

This is the meaning of our sages' saying (*Berachot* 30b) that "One should not rise to pray but with *koved rosh* ('heaviness of the head;' humility)"[5]: when one prays with *kavanah*, the Holy One, blessed is He, is glorified in the "World of Speech." This brings glorification into all worlds, and also upon [the one who prays]. Thus he must be careful not to cease from the *deveikut* (attachment [to God]), i.e., he should not think of self-glorification on account of praying with great *kavanah*.

The *beinunim* (intermediate) are those who in prayer have in mind also that the Holy One, blessed is He, grant them the

---

level. (*Cf.* above, sect. 73.) "When man attaches himself to the words [of speech], they intercede on his behalf. This happens if his sole intent is but to join the 'World of Speech' to the 'World of Thought.'" (*Maggid Devarav Leya'akov*, sect. 58, which is a brief version of this section.)

3. I.e., notwithstanding what was said above, note 2, that the prayer will then be answered.

4. [A stirring (initiative) from below, effects a reciprocal stirring from Above; *Zohar* I:77b and 86b, II:31b *et passim* (and see below, sect. 142).]

"One must believe that as soon as the prayer has been uttered, one is answered for what has been requested. It may be asked, that at times the fulfillment of the request is not perceived. In fact, however, [the prayer has been answered, except that] this is concealed from the petitioner . . . in terms of the universe as a whole." (*Keter Shem Tov*, sect. 80) All prayers are effective in the upper worlds, and sometimes in other parts of the universe. Their effect is according to what omniscient God determines to be for the best interests of man and the world. Thus man must beware never to assume that his prayers are of no avail. (*Ibid.*, sect. 138 and 145; and see there also sect. 81, 176 and 214.)

5. This Talmudic statement is explained above, sect. 73, see there.

request of their mundane needs. They "remain suspended[6] from Rosh Hashanah until Yom Kippur" (*Rosh Hashanah* 16b), i.e., the "World of Thought" which is referred to as Yom Kippur.[7] This means, the suspension remains until [the examination of] the "thought," i.e., their *kavanah* (intent): if their intent in requesting mundane needs is for the sake of Heaven, to free them for the service [of God], blessed be He, they, too, shall be inscribed for life.[8] For the "World of Speech" and the "World of Thought" are unified by virtue of their *kavanah*.

[The phrase] "three books" denotes [forms of] speech.[9]

---

6. I.e., unlike the perfectly righteous, who are inscribed for life immediately on Rosh Hashanah, the judgment of the intermediate is suspended until Yom Kippur.

7. Yom Kippur is identified with *Binah* (*Zohar Chadash, Tikunim* 93b), the "World of Thought." See also *Zohar* II:185a and III:100bff.

8. The *beinunim's* service is not as great as that of the perfectly righteous whose concern is exclusively *tzorech gevohah* (for the purely spiritual effects on high). The intermediate worry also about their own needs on earth; but when they do so not for self-indulgence, but for the sake of Heaven, this, too, is meritorious and acceptable, and they are inscribed for life.

"The intermediate, whose intent is [not only] to unify, but also that the Holy One, blessed is He, grant them their [personal] wish, stand suspended until Yom Kippurim; for then there is a manifestation of the 'World of Thought' and every thought ascends. Thus their thought, too, will be effective." (*Maggid Devarav Leya'akov*, sect. 58)

9. The term *sefer* (book) is an idiom of *siper* (relate; communicate), thus speech. See *Sefer Yetzirah* 1:1, and the commentaries thereon.

124

"These are the *shemot* (names) of the children of Israel [coming to *Mitzrayim* (Egypt) . . . Reuben, Shimon, Levi . . .]." (Exodus 1:1-2)

R. Israel Baal Shem, his memory is for a blessing, for the life of the world to come, [interpreted] the verses "They

turned Jerusalem into heaps (of rubble); they have given the
nivlat (the corpse) of *avadecha* (Your servants) as food to the
birds of the sky, [the flesh of Your devoted ones to the beasts
of the earth]" (Psalms 79:1-2):

Galut (exile) came about in this world by our many sins
because "they turned *Yerushalayim* (Jerusalem) into heaps (of
rubble)."[1] That is, when a person attained some fear [of God],
or some perfection, by the performance of a *mitzvah*, this leads
him to a sense of pride. This is the meaning of "they turned
[*Yerushalayim*]"—their *yirah-shalem* (perfect fear)[2]—"into
heaps," i.e., into a large, high pile.[3] When performing a [good]
deed, as of Torah or prayer and so forth, he turns it into a *nevel*
(lyre) and harp; that is, he does so not with fear and love, but
as one playing the lyre.[4] This causes, his *avodah* (service of
God) to move—Heaven forbid—to the *kelipot* (forces of evil).[5]
Thus it is written, "as food for the birds of the sky," which denotes the *kelipot*. What caused this? The fact that he turned his
deed into a *nevel* (lyre). This is the meaning of "*nivlat avadecha*
as food for the birds of the sky . . . to the beasts of the earth."

In the same vein one can interpret [our text] "These are
the *shemot* (names) . . .": What caused the *galut* and the *shima-*

---

1. I.e., the destruction of Jerusalem is not the effect but the *cause*. As the sequel
explains, this refers to the spiritual Jerusalem.
2. The term *Yerushalayim* is a compound of *yirah* (fear) and *shalem* (whole; perfect); *Bereishit Rabba* 56:10; *Midrash Tehilim* 76:3. Thus it signifies the aspects
of fear of God and perfection in the service of God.
3. I.e., into self-elevation, pride and arrogance.
4. I.e., an idiomatic interpretation of *nivlat avadecha*: the deeds in the Divine
service (of those who ostensibly are "Your servants"), are turned into self-
serving musical instruments.
5. I.e., it will not ascend on high, but descend to the *kelipot*. Moreover, by descending to the *kelipot* it will strengthen them as well (see above, sect. 87).

mon (desolation; appalment)[6] of the "coming to *Mitzrayim* (Egypt)," i.e., into the *meitzar* (straits)[7] of the *galut*? The answer is: "Reuben," i.e., when performing a deed he says to himself "*re'u* (see) the difference between me and other people;[8] for I perform my service [of God] perfectly, and it is only fit that God, may He be blessed, *yishma* (hear) my voice[9] and *yilaveh* (attach Himself) to me,"[10] as alluded in [the names] Shimon [and Levi]; and likewise with the other names.[11]

6. I.e., reading *shemot* as an idiom of *shamah* (desolation; appalment); *Berachot* 7b.

7. I.e., reading *Mitzrayim* as an idiom of *meitzar* (distress; straits); *Bereishit Rabba* 16:4. In our context this relates specifically to the *galut* of Egypt, but it applies to every *galut* as this is a generic term for every exile (*ibid.*). See also above, sect. 64, note 4.

8. The name Reuben is rooted in the word *ra'ah* (to see); Genesis 29:32. Moreover, Leah, his mother, had in mind: "*Re'u-ben*—see the difference between my [first-born] son and the son of my mother-in-law (i.e., Esau)." (*Berachot* 7b) Here, though, this (and the subsequent interpretations) are taken in the negative sense; see below, note 10.

9. The name Shimon is rooted in the word *shama* (to hear): "God heard." (Genesis 29:33)

10. The name Levi is rooted in the word *lavah* (to join; to attach): "My husband will become attached to me." (Genesis 29:34)

11. Everything in holiness has a counterpart in impurity (see above, sect. 13, note 2). Thus "just as the names of the tribes appear in holiness, so, too, they have a counter-part in *kelipah*;" *Keter Shem Tov*, sect. 31 and 403 (see there).

125

"A righteous person will flourish like a date-palm, grow tall like a cedar in Lebanon." (Psalms 92:13)

There are two types of *tzadikim* (righteous people), and both are perfectly righteous. The difference between them is as follows:

One is in a continuous state of *deveikut* (attachment) to God and performs the service incumbent upon him. He is a *tzadik*, however, just for himself, and not for others. That is, he does not make his righteousness affect others. He is the one who is compared to a cedar of which our sages, of blessed memory, said that it does not bear fruits. (*Ta'anit* 25b) For he is a *tzadik* just to himself and does not produce fruits, i.e., bringing others back to goodness so that *tzadikim* may multiply and be fruitful in the world. He is concerned but about himself, to "grow tall" and enhance his reward.

The second type of *tzadik* is compared to a date-palm, which produces fruits: "he will flourish like a date-palm," that is, he "brings out the precious from the vile" (Jeremiah 15:19), he causes goodness to flourish and multiply in the world.

Our sages, of blessed memory, thus said that "the perfect *tzadikim* cannot stand in the place where the *ba'alei teshuvah* (penitent) stand." (*Berachot* 34b) That is, this second type of *tzadik* is called *ba'al teshuvah*, i.e., he is the *proprietor and master of teshuvah*.[1] For he restores others to goodness, "turned many away from iniquity" (Malachi 2:6), and effected *teshuvah* in the world. His reward is doubled and redoubled far beyond that of the first type of *tzadik*,[2] though the latter, too, is perfectly righteous.[3]

---

1. This interpretation of the term *ba'al teshuvah* in the literal sense of "master (in Kabbalistic context: 'husband') of *teshuvah*," appears in *Zohar* II:106b. (This concept of the *tzadik* as *ba'al teshuvah* is discussed at length in R. Mosheh de Tirani, *Bet Elokim, Sha'ar Hateshuvah*, ch. 3.) In this context, the *tzadik* becomes the cause of *teshuvah* of the wicked; see *Keter Shem Tov*, sect. 270; and the Maggid's *Or Torah*, No'ach, sect. 15, and *Aggadot*, sect. 486, 487 and 489.

2. See *Zohar* II:128b: "The worthy person must pursue the wicked to remove from him the filth [of sin] and to subdue the *sitra achara*.. This is a praiseworthy act effecting an exaltation of the Holy One, blessed is He, more than from any other praiseworthy act, and this exaltation is greater than all oth-

ers.. Come and see: whoever takes the hand of the wicked and induces him to forsake his evil way, rises with three ascents unlike any other person." (see the sequel there and on the next page). Note the Baal Shem Tov's interpretation of this passage in *Keter Shem Tov*, sect. 113 and 251 (and see there also sect. 131 and 389), cautioning that the wicked must be restored to goodness with empathy and kindness.

3. *Cf.* the differentiations between Noah, Abraham and Moses in *Zohar* I:67b, 106a and 254b; and also in *Devarim Rabba* 11:3.

126-127

This, too, is an important principle:

When you think of performing a *mitzvah*, do not refrain from doing it for [fear of a sense of] pride or whatever ulterior motive related to it. For, as known, "Out of [acting] *shelo lishmah* (not for its own sake) [one comes (to act) *lishmah* (for its own sake)]." (*Pesachim* 50b)[1] The very act of a good deed already effects on high a good vessel, and the inwardness of the vessel is produced by the intent.[2]

First of all must be the [good; proper] choice.[3] After this choice you must see to it that "your mouth and heart harmonize"[4] to believe with absolute faith, without any ulterior thought, that "the whole earth is full of His glory" (Isaiah 6:3) and that everything is possessed of His vital force, blessed be

1. Up to here is a brief restatement of the principle stated above, sect. 55.
2. The performance of a *mitzvah* has an objective validity on its own, even if the proper intent is as yet lacking: the action on its own is like the "body" of the *mitzvah* (or its effects), while the *kavanah* (the person's proper intent) is its soul (*cf.* above, sect. 58 and 116). Thus first of all submit to your obligations and do the *mitzvah*. The emphasis on *kavanah* and *deveikut* is never meant to over-ride the Halachic obligations. (See above, sect. 55, note 1; and *cf.* also *Keter Shem Tov*, sect. 47.)
3. I.e., choosing to act, to perform the *mitzvah*.
4. I.e., to make an effort to harmonize (lit., "make as one") your thought and intent with the act of performing a Divine precept.

He.[5] Thus every form of love, fear and all the other attributes—even the bad things in the world[6]—all come from Him, blessed be He. Thus you are not permitted to love, fear, glorify, or make prevail[7] anything beyond Him, blessed be He; and likewise with all the other attributes.

Whenever you are afraid of something, or love it, you ought to consider: "Whence is this present fear or love? After all, everything derives from Him, blessed be He, who put the [aspects of] fear and love even in bad things, such as wild beasts. For at the time of the 'breaking [of the vessels]'[8] something fell from all the attributes. The fear, therefore, is from Him, blessed be He. Why, then, should I be afraid of a single spark of His which is [vested] in that bad thing? It is better to attach myself to the 'great fear'! The same applies to love, and so, too, with all the attributes, to extract the spark [of holiness] from there and raise it to its root.[9] For this is the ultimate desire of our soul, to raise [the fallings of] the 'breaking [of the vessels]'[10] to their source."[11]

The same applies to your speech: do not think that it is *you* who speaks. Rather, it is the vital force within you, which de-

---

5. See above, sect. 84, 90 and 119.—The consciousness of Divine omnipresence, and of the fact that everything exists but by virtue of its Divine vitality, will of itself lead to the proper attitude and intent. *Cf.* above, sect. 58.

6. See below, sect. 130. *Cf. Keter Shem Tov*, sect. 26: "The *Shechinah* compounds all worlds, [all of] the inorganic, the vegetative, animals, and humans, and all creatures, the good and the bad . . . for the bad is but a base for the good." See also *ibid.*, sect. 70, 106,188 and 396.

7. Corresponding to the attributes of *Chessed, Gevurah, Tiferet* and *Netzach* (see above, sect. 87).

8. See above, sect. 120, note 4.

9. See above, sect. 119.

10. See above, sect. 120, note 4.

11. This is again the principle of sublimating man's emotive attributes or traits to holiness, as already discussed above, sect. 14, 22, 87, 90, 101 and 120.

rives from the Creator, blessed is He, that speaks through you and raises the speech to its source.[12] This [attitude] compounds also the [notion of] equanimity,[13] because the faculty of speech is the same in another as it is with you, for all derives from Him, blessed be He.[14]

Likewise when eating, your intent should be to extract the vitality [from the food] to elevate it to Above through the service of the Creator, blessed be He. And so, too, with everything else.[15] Your intent in everything should be to effect that you attach yourself to Above.[16]

---

12. See above, sect. 88, 103 and 120.
13. See above, sect. 2 and 10.
14. *Cf.* above, sect. 12.
15. See above, sect. 109.
16. *Cf.* above, sect. 2-3.

128

The reason why [both] love and fear [are necessary]: If man had only love of God, he would be accustomed to being continuously with God.[1] Moreover, the love would be so impressed upon him that it would become his very nature.[2] By virtue of fear joined to [the love], however, he will be afraid to approach.[3]

---

1. I.e., he would lose the sense of reverence, for familiarity breeds contempt. "He who acts with love [only] . . . will sometimes not sense to act scrupulously. The one who has a sense of fear, however, will carefully watch to act properly." *Likkutim Yekarim*, end of sect. 118); and see there also sect. 42 (with greater elaboration in the Maggid's *Or Torah*, Vayechi, sect. 59); and *Maggid Devarav Leya'akov*, sect. 115.

2. I.e., it would no longer be appreciated, for "continuous pleasure is no pleasure" (see above, sect. 111).

3. See *Keter Shem Tov*, sect. 349, and *Maggid Devarav Leya'akov*, sect. 7 and 203, explaining how the seemingly contrary feelings of love and fear can be

joined in the service of God. See also above, sect. 110 with regards to compounding fear and joy.

129

To understand what is *katnut* ("smallness;" constricted consciousness) and what is *gadlut* ("greatness;" expanded consciousness):

When a person sits and studies Torah, for example, and does so without discernment, he is in a state of *katnut*; his mind is not complete. On the other hand, when he studies with discernment and *hitlahavut* (fervor; enthusiasm) he is on the level of *gadlut*, because he is attached to the supernal levels.

The [states of] *katnut* and *gadlut* relate likewise to prayer and every *mitzvah* performed by man.[1]

---

1. See above, sect. 67, 69 and 96, and below, sect. 135 and 137.

130

One might wonder: In context of the creation, the Torah states several times ["it was good;" and at the conclusion thereof (Genesis 1:31)] "and behold it was very good." In the Book of Deuteronomy, however, it is written, "See, I have placed before you life and the good, and death and the evil." (Deuteronomy 30:15) Where did the evil come from?

One cannot interpret this in line with our speaking of real evil.[1] [In actuality,] the "evil," too, is good, except that it is the

---

1. Evil cannot be a real entity on its own, independent of (and opposed to) goodness and holiness, for that would imply the heresy of dualism. By the same token one cannot say that there is real evil, albeit created by God: God is the very essence of pure goodness, thus only good can come from Him. Yet we do experience evil on earth, and, as said, the Torah itself states "I have placed before you.. death and the evil." What then is that which we call evil?

lowest level of absolute good.[2] This is alluded in the *Zohar's* reference to "*mile'eil umile'ra*—from above and from below."[3]

---

2. All that God created is good. By means of *tzimtzum* (Divine Self-contraction), a process of devolution brought about crude matter and the lowest entities to be found on earth. The source and core of all beings, however, is pure spirituality, absolute good. Without the Divine spark inherent in all beings, they could not exist. Thus even those things that are forbidden and condemned by the Torah, and constitute that which we call evil, are rooted in Divine goodness. They came about to enable man's self-realization by proving him with the options of free choice ("life and the good" vs. "death and the evil"). The things the Torah calls evil are truly evil relative to ourselves. In their origin (and their intended purpose), however, they are really good.

This principle is explained in terms of a popular parable in the *Zohar* II:163a: A king provided his son with the best education and instructions to lead an exemplary moral life. To test his son's obedience and devotion, he hired a beautiful and clever woman and ordered her to seduce the prince. That woman used every blandishment to tempt the prince, but he rejected her allurements. Needless to say, this brought great joy to the king and he rewarded his son with precious gifts and honors. Now, who was instrumental in bringing all that glory to the prince? None other but the temptress! Thus she is to be praised on all counts: she fulfilled the king's orders, and through her the prince became worthy of his rewards and an intensified love from his father. (*Cf.* also below, sect. 138.)

That which we call evil, therefore, is, in effect, a "base (lit., "seat") for good" (see above, sect. 126-127, note 6). In essence, in terms of its origin (and purpose), it is good. As it descends to its mundane manifestation, however, the good is altogether concealed and invisible, and all we see is but the truly evil shell.

3. The reference appears to be to *Zohar* I:49b which discusses how things *below* are rooted in the spiritual categories of *above*: the *yetzer hara* has a spiritual source, it is rooted in goodness *above*, but it itself becomes manifest in evil *below*.

The terms *mile'eil* and *milera* do not actually appear there, but are synonymous with the terms in that passage. They lend themselves to our context: *milera* (from below) is interpreted as an expression of *ra* (evil); that is, "from below" it is "evil," though *mile'eil* (from above) it is really good. See also below, sect. 132, note 7.

Thus when effecting good, the evil, too, becomes good.[4] But when sinning, Heaven forbid, it becomes real evil.[5] Take, for example, a broom for sweeping the house: in context of clearing the house it has some good quality. It [may be] a low level, but it is still good. But when it is used to hit a child doing some wrong, the broom becomes truly evil when hitting the child.[6]

---

4. See above, note 2.
5. The kelipot (i.e., the realm of evil) exist only by virtue of the Divine will. They are sustained by sparks of holiness deeply embedded within them, albeit in limited measure that is just sufficient for their intended purpose. When man sins, however, he infuses additional vitality and energy into the kelipot (see above, sect. 9) which empowers them to go beyond tempting man, to try and "conquer and prevail with full force." Thus it becomes real evil.
6. The broom per se is morally neutral. In essence it is mere potentiality: when used for good, its potential for good is realized and confers goodness upon itself. When used for evil, its potential for evil is realized and confers evil upon itself.

131

"All the days of the poor are bad." (Proverbs 15:15)

Our sages said, "No one is poor except for him who lacks knowledge." (Nedarim 41a) In this context, [our text] means the following: "All the days of the poor"—in knowledge—"are bad," because his prayer and Torah-study are not considered at all before [God], blessed be He. For surely they are devoid of fear and love, thus they do not ascend on high.[1]

But the question is raised : "There are the Sabbaths and festivals?" (Ketuvot 110b)[2] That is, surely in these days there is

---

1. Torah studied without fear and love does not ascend on high. (Tikunei Zohar 10:25b) This applies to prayer as well; see above, sect. 87.
2. I.e., how can you say that "all the days of the poor are bad" when there are the Sabbaths and festivals when even the poor are provided with good food?

a "stirring from Above" unto man, and he will certainly pray on these with devotion?[3] The answer is : "A change of diet [is the beginning of bowel-disease]." (*Ibid.*) That is, though he does pray now with devotion, and regards himself as praying with devotion, this leads him to pride and a sense of greatness, imagining himself to have ascended now to a sublime level.[4] Thus even now [his days] are bad. For "a change of diet is the beginning of bowel-disease;" that is, "the *yetzer hara* is provoked only by eating and drinking" (*Zohar* I:110a) and that is what led him to pride. And a word to the wise is sufficient.

---

3. Just as there is a beneficial change on Sabbaths and festivals in terms of physical food, so, too, it is in terms of "spiritual food": on the Sabbaths and festivals there is a manifestation of holiness, "the *Shechinah* never departs from Israel on the Sabbaths and festivals" (*Zohar* III:179b; and see there also I:75b: "On the Sabbath.. all [the *kelipot*] are removed and have no dominion.. and the world is in joy and is sustained from [holiness].") See also above, sect. 85.

4. I.e., the special condition of the Sabbaths and festivals will lead him to a sense of self-satisfaction, and the error of imagining that he need not improve. God must be served *every* day. (See above, sect. 85.) The service restricted to Sabbaths and festivals, albeit elevated, thus proves counterproductive. *Cf.* above, sect. 74.

132

An interpretation of the verse in Psalms [which reads]: "I will thank God with all my heart, I will relate all Your wondrous works." (Psalms 9:2)

The plain sense of this verse requires careful consideration. Granted that the phrase "I will thank God with all my heart" is well and good. The verse's conclusion, however, "I will relate all Your wondrous works," presents a difficulty. Is it not written (Psalms 106:2) "Who can express the mighty acts of God, make all of His praise to be heard?!" Thus how could he say "I will relate *all* of Your wondrous works?"

This can be explained in context of the *Zohar's* comment
[on the verse (Genesis 22:1)] "And God *nissah* (tested) *et Avraham* (lit. "the Abraham;" Abraham)," that it should have said
"*nissah leAvraham*—tested Abraham" [without the particle *et*].
(*Zohar* 119b) This will be understood in view of the well-
known premise that *chessed* (love; kindness) is the attribute of
Abraham, as it is said, "*chessed* unto Abraham." (Micah 7:20)[1]

Our Sages, of blessed memory, said (*Chulin* 91b) that there
are angels who recite hymns only once every seven years, and
according to some only once every fifty years. Their recitals
are brief: some say [but the single word] *kadosh* (holy);[2] some
say "*baruch*—blessed be"[3]. (*Ibid.*) Some [angels] say one verse,
as it is said of certain angels that each of them recites one verse
from the psalm "Thank God, for He is good." (Psalms 136);[4]
and so forth. Any one of Israel, however, is allowed to speak
and laud at any time and occasion, and to prolong this with
every kind of laudations, songs and praises.[5]

This will be understood with the parable of a king, all of
whose servants and ministers came to recite hymns before him
and to laud him. Now each one is allotted a certain time and
limit for his laudation, corresponding to the individual's rank
and importance. Moreover, all this happens [only] when the
king is favorably inclined. If, however, the king is in an angry
mood, Heaven forbid, they are afraid to laud him at all, as it is
said, "How can you laud the King at a time of wrath?" (*Kinot
for the Ninth of Av*) When apprehensive because of doubt
whether the king is angry, Heaven forbid, or lest he become

---

1. See above, sect. 87, note 11.
2. I.e., of the verse "Holy, holy, holy is God." (Isaiah 6:3)
3. Ezekiel 3:12
4. See *Siddur R. Isaac Luria*, ed. R. Shabtai of Rashkov, *s.v. Shacharit LeShabbat*
   (p. 70b), listing the respective angels reciting each verse.
5. See *Chulin* 91b.

angry for whatever reason, they would be as brief as possible and immediately leave his presence. On the other hand, when the king's beloved and loving son enters to laud [his father], he is not concerned about all that. For even if the king is angry, seeing his beloved son enter effects joy and delight in the father.

Now, we said that anger departs with the advent of joy and love. To be sure, this is only natural. Nonetheless, we must understand why this is so. It can be explained [as follows]: When love and joy prevail, they cause the anger and wrath to ascend to their source above where they are "sweetened;" for, as known, "*dinim* (judgments; severe decrees) can be sweetened only at their root."[6]

This, then, is the meaning of the verse "And *Elokim* (God) *nissah et Avraham*": *Elokim*, which denotes *dinim*,[7] *nissah*—was made to ascend;[8] i.e., they departed all the way to above and

---

6. A basic Kabbalistic premise; see R. Chaim Vital, *Eitz Chayim* 13:1; and *Mikdash Melech* on *Zohar* I:151a.

   In the human or earthly experience of *dinim*, they are "bad": they are manifest in suffering. They originate in the Divine attribute of *Gevurah*, which itself is rooted in the *Sefirah* of *Binah*. The Divine attributes, however, are altogether good. The root and source of *dinim*, therefore, is good, and their ultimate purpose is for good as well, except that they devolve to their mundane manifestation and perception as something bad or evil. (See above, sect. 130.) The consciousness of their true nature, realizing their inherent goodness ("Whatever the Merciful does is for good"—*Berachot* 60b) thus traces the evil below to its goodness above, and this effects a "sweetening of the judgment in its source": the evil is annulled and its intended goodness becomes manifest. See *Keter Shem Tov*, sect. 33.

7. See above, sect. 102, note 1.

8. The word *nissah*, generally translated "tested," also means "elevated; raised" (as in Isaiah 30:17, 49:22 and 62:10; see *Mechilta* and *Lekach Tov* on Exodus 20:17, cited by Rashi *ad loc.*). These two meanings converge in the fact that every test is for the purpose of elevation. Thus in our context, too, both meanings are given to "God *nissah* Abraham"—see *Bereishit Rabba*, ch. 55, and *Zohar* I:140a.

were sweetened. Why? [Because of] "*et Avraham*,"[9] that is, by virtue of the love and *chessed* (kindness) signified by Abraham who is compared to the King's son.[10]

Let us return to the above parable. We said that the son lauds without restriction. For a son is obligated to praise his father to no end and limit for two reasons. First of all, he is his father and king, thus obligating him to offer thanks and to praise exceedingly, especially as he has no reason to be apprehensive [as stated above]. Moreover, the very fact that he, unlike any other minister and marshal, was granted permission to laud beyond any limit, is itself reason to praise his father, the king. For the offering of thanks applies whenever one is granted some additional privilege from Above, as it is said with the birth of Judah, "And Leah said, This time let me [gratefully] praise [God]." (Genesis 29:35)[11]

Our text may then possibly read as follows: "I will thank God with all my heart;" that is, aside of the fact that I am duty-bound to offer praise and laudation [unto God] because of the filial obligation to a father, I will thank Him also because "God is in all my heart." That is to say, the love for [God], blessed be He, is firmly inserted in my heart; this, in turn, indicates that [His] love for me, too, is firmly inserted in *His* heart, for "as water (reflects) face to face, [so is the heart of man to man]." (Proverbs 27:19) For this very reason He permitted me to "relate all Your wondrous works."

---

9. I.e., "*with* Abraham."

10. I.e., the *dinim* (signified by *Elokim*) were made to ascend and become sweetened, *with* (by virtue of) the attribute of *Chessed* (signified by "Abraham").

11. Leah assumed that her share would be three of the twelve sons of Jacob. As she gave birth to a fourth son, thus *more* than her share, she expressed special gratitude. (*Tanchuma*, Vayeitze:9; *Bereishit Rabba* 7:4; cited by Rashi *ad loc.*)

As for [the difficulty from the verse] "Who can express [the mighty acts of God].. ," this is [resolved by the phrase] "I shall relate." That is, the little that I am able to [gratefully] praise and relate should be accounted as if I related "*all* Your wondrous works." The hindrance [of inability] is not on my part: it is simply impossible to complete the praise of the Master of the Universe and to relate "*all* Your wondrous works," because there is no limit and end to them. Thus whatever "I will relate," i.e., the little one is able to relate, shall be accounted as if it would be *all* of His wondrous works. For I am obligated to relate His praise beyond limit because of the two reasons cited above.

133

"Whoever engages in excessive talk brings on *cheit* (sin)." (*Avot* 1:17) [The term *cheit*] denotes deficiency.[1] Even when speaking with others words of the wisdom of the Torah, silence is much more preferable. For in silence one can think of the greatness of [God], blessed be He, and join oneself unto Him, blessed be He, more so than the joining by means of speech.[2]

Sometimes one can be lying in bed, and to others it appears that he is sleeping, but at that very time he is actually in solitude with the Creator, blessed be He.[3]

---

1. This meaning for *cheit* appears in Genesis 31:39; Judges 20:16; and I Kings 1:21. See Rashi on Genesis 31:39.

2. *Cf. Likkutim Yekarim*, sect. 190: "'Silence is a fence for wisdom' (*Avot* 3:13) because in silence one is able to become attached to the World of Thought which is [the *Sefirah*] of *Chochmah* (Wisdom)."

   The parallel version of our text in *Hanhagot Yesharot* adds (in brackets) that this applies only to one who has attained an exalted level of spirituality. For all others it is preferable that they engage in words of Torah. *Cf.* above, sect. 65.

3. *Cf.* above, sect. 105.

134

[The ability] to always see the Creator, blessed be He, with the mental eye, even as one looks upon another person, is a high level [of attainment]. Bear in mind that when you are continuously with pure and clear thought, then the Creator, blessed be He, too, is looking upon you just as another person does.[1]

1. See below, sect. 137; and *cf. Keter Shem Tov*, sect. 169.—The parallel version of our text in *Likkutim Yekarim*, sect. 209 (and *Keter Shem Tov*, sect. 232) reads: "Bear in mind that the Creator, blessed be He, too, is looking upon you just as another person does. This shall be in your mind constantly, with a pure, clear and lucid thought."

135

At first attach yourself properly unto the Creator, blessed be He, below, and then you will be able to ascend to Above.[1]

You will have to descend several times during the day, to below, in order to rest a little from your thought.[2] At times you can serve only with *katnut* (restricted consciousness[3]), and will not be able to ascend on high.[4]

1. *Cf.* above, sect. 32 and 69; below, sect. 136 and 143; and *Keter Shem Tov*, sect. 281.
2. *Cf.* above, sect. 67, especially note 1.
3. For the concept of *katnut* see above, sect. 129.
4. See above, sect. 69, and *cf.* below, sect. 137.

136

Some times you are able to attach yourself to Above even when you are not praying. [You can do so] by thinking that you are beyond the dome of the firmament, and then strengthen yourself to ascend even higher.[1]

Some times you are unable to ascend to Above even during prayer, and you serve with [fear and] love below.[2] By virtue of speaking below with fear and love, and attaching yourself to the Creator, blessed be He, you will have the strength to ascend beyond all the Firmaments and Thrones, the *Ofanim* and the *Seraphim*,[3] and to speak there in that realm.

---

1. For man is where his thought is; see above, sect. 69.
2. See above, sect. 67.
3. I.e., beyond the Worlds of *Asiyah, Yetzirah* and *Atzilut* which correspond to the categories of "the Firmaments and Thrones, the *Ofanim* and the *Seraphim*." *Cf.* below, sect. 137 and 143.

137

Bear in mind about the Creator that "the whole earth is full of His glory" (Isaiah 6:3) and His *Shechinah* is constantly at your side.[1] He is "ultimate fineness." He is the Master of all actions in the world, and He can effect whatever [you] may desire. Thus it is only proper for you to trust in Him alone, blessed be He.[2]

Think that you look at the *Shechinah* which is at your side just as you look at physical objects.[3] This is a service [of God] on the level of *katnut* (smallness; constricted consciousness).[4]

Some times you are able to discern that there are yet many spheres [over you], but you stand on the small dot that is the earth. The whole universe is as naught in relation to the Creator, blessed be He, Who is *En Sof* (Infinite). He effected a

---

1. See above, sect. 84.
2. See above, sect. 24.
3. See above, sect. 134.
4. See above, sect. 67.

tzimtzum (Self-constriction), "clearing" within Himself a space in which to create the worlds.[5] You may understand this intellectually, but you are still unable to ascend to the supernal worlds. This is the meaning of "God appeared to me from afar" (Jeremiah 31:2), i.e., seeing God from afar.

On the other hand, when you serve [God] on the level of *gadlut* (greatness; expanded consciousness),[6] you strengthen yourself with great force and ascend in thought, penetrating all firmaments in one swoop and ascending higher than the angels, the *Ofanim*, the *Seraphim* and the Thrones.[7] This is perfect worship.

Always be joyful.[8] Think and believe with perfect faith that the *Shechinah* is at your side and watches over you. You look at the Creator, blessed be He, and the Creator, blessed be He, looks at you.[9] The Creator, blessed be He, can do anything He desires. If He wills it, He can destroy all the worlds in a single instant and create them in a single instant. In Him, blessed be He, are rooted all the good things and the judgments in the world, for His effluence and vitality is in all things.[10] Thus "I trust only in Him, and fear Him alone, blessed be He."

---

5. See above, sect. 84.
6. See above, sect. 129.
7. See above, end of sect. 136.
8. See above, sect. 15, 44-46, 107 and 110.
9. See above, sect. 134.
10. See above, sect. 130.

138

"God is great and much praised, in the City of our God, His holy mountain." (Psalms 48:2)

This may be interpreted in context of the verse, "Israel, in whom I shall be glorified" (Isaiah 49:3): God derives much glory, delight and pleasure from the *tzadik's* deeds, his Torah and prayer. Our sages, of blessed memory, state: "[The Holy One, blessed is He, says to Israel: 'My children,] I have created the *yetzer hara*, and I created the Torah as its *tavlin* ("spices;" antidote).'" (*Kidushin* 30b) This is to say: "Your love and affection for us is very great! You created the *yetzer hara* and You created the Torah. Thus you gave us the strength to overcome the *yetzer hara* and to 'sweeten' it by means of the Torah, even as spices are used in cooking. It follows, then, that everything is from You. All we accomplished is from You and from Your power. Nonetheless, you take great delight in it, and You take pride in us, as if we had done it by the might of our own hands.[1] This manifests the fierce love, and the additional affection that was made known to us, in calling us 'children of the Omnipresent' (*Avot* 3:18)."

It is like a child dearly loved by his father, visited by a guest who came to examine him. [The boy] had no understanding at all of the legal ruling [on which he was to be tested] because of its great profundity and subtlety. The father, for his great affection for him, could not bear his beloved son's anguish at being confounded and unable to understand. What did the father do? He provided him with an opening to that ruling, showing him a way to follow, so that he would be able

---

1. All of man's achievements are possible only by virtue of God providing him with the possibility and energy to do them. In effect, then, man should not get any credit for these. Nonetheless, God accounts it to man as if he had accomplished it on his own. This resolves the apparent contradiction in the verse "You, God, have kindness, for you reward man in accordance with his deeds" (Psalms 62:13)": "Kindness" implies gratuitous grace; to "reward man in accordance with his deeds" implies well-deserved compensation, thus not something gratuitous! However, though it is only by Divine grace that man has the ability and opportunity to do good, God in His kindness rewards him as if he had done it on his own. (*Likkutim Yekarim*, sect. 110; *Keter Shem Tov*, sect. 191-193, and end of 354, and *cf. ibid.* sect. 55.)

to discuss it properly. He just about informed him of the full content of the ruling.

Now the guest came to ask [the son] about the ruling and to test him in front of his father. [The son] started to recite the ruling and the visitor asked him several questions, raising a number of difficulties. He answered appropriately, offering objections and resolving them, with a clear and brilliant mind. His father is joyful, delighted and proud seeing this. [The father knows that the son's] achievement was wholly due to himself. Nonetheless, he has great pleasure [from it].

Moreover, as the visitor notes the father's pleasure, he wants to enhance it further. Thus he prevails over the boy with additional questions, raising numerous new and complex difficulties. The son, however, trusting in his father, bestirs himself on his own to be wise, and resolves all difficulties.

This is the meaning of their saying that "he who is greater than another, his *yetzer [hara]* is greater than the other's." (*Sukah* 52a) Also, our sages, of blessed memory, said: "Satan acted for the sake of Heaven." (*Baba Bathra* 16a)[2] The moral is clearly understood. For when [Satan, i.e., the *yetzer hara*] sees that the *tzadik* subdues him, and that this causes delight unto God, he strengthens himself against [the *tzadik*] every day,[3] and [the *tzadik*] subdues, and prevails over, his *yetzer [hara]*.

Our Sages, of blessed memory, thus said that "the Holy One, blessed is He, called Jacob *Eil*." (*Megilah* 18a) *Eil* denotes strength and might,[4] as in "He took away the *eilei* (mighty) of the land." (Ezekiel 17:13) This is the meaning of "He called him *Eil*," because the *tzadik* is referred to as "the mighty who subdues his *yetzer [hara]*." (*Avot* 4:1) In the time to come, our

---

2. I.e., he serves the purpose of testing man, as in the parable cited above, sect. 130, note 2.
3. *Cf. Sukah* 52b.
4. See *Zohar* III:132a.

sages, of blessed memory, say, the *yetzer hara* "will seem to the righteous to look like a tall mountain" (*Sukah* 52a), and the might of the righteous in subduing so tall a mountain will be recognized, manifest and made famous to all.

In the time to come, perhaps all will refer to the *tzadikim* with the name *Eil*. This is alluded in the verse "As now, it is said [to Jacob and to] Israel, 'What has *Eil* wrought?'" (Numbers 23:23) It is known that "Israel" is a term for the *tzadik*.[5] Thus it is written: "As now, it is said . . . to Israel," i.e., to the *tzadik*, saying to him "What has *Eil* wrought?" That is, the *tzadik* is asked, "What have you, *Eil*, wrought?," just as one inquires after the well-being of another in terms of "You, 'so-and-so,' what do you do, and how are you?"

The sequence of the text thus reads as follows:

"God is great and much praised." That is, it is incumbent upon us to magnify and praise Him for all the good He bestows upon us. For all the greatness and glory that He, blessed be He, derives from our worship is altogether *"be'ir Elokeinu* (in the City of our God)": *be'ir* is an expression of *hit'orerut* (stirring; awakening),[6] [thus reading *be'ir Elokeinu* as "by virtue of the stirring] by our God." For He is the one who bestirs us and gives us the strength to serve Him and to prevail, as our Sages, of blessed memory said: "If the Holy One, blessed is He, would not help [man], [he could not overcome (the *yetzer hara*).]" (*Sukah* 52b) Nonetheless, He, blessed be He, still has pleasure and pride, and gives us a great reward, rewarding us as if we had done everything on our own.

---

5. See the reference to Isaiah 49:3 at the beginning of this section. In *Maggid Devarav Leya'akov*, sect. 250, this is stated more explicitly: "'Israel in whom I shall be glorified' refers to the *tzadikim*, for His glory, blessed be He, comes about by means of their good deeds and their *deveikut* in God."

6. This interpretation for the word *ir* is found already in *Targum Yehonathan* on Numbers 21:27.

In fact, however, the true service is something that has to come by virtue of our own stirring.[7] We are "a part of God from on high;"[8] thus [our service should be] *be'ir* (by the stirring) of our *yetzer [hatov]*, i.e., the portion of Divinity within us—"*Elokeinu—our* God."[9]

---

7. I.e., to take the initiative on his own in order to deserve what comes his way. One is not to rely on gratuitous gifts (which the Talmud refers to as "bread of shame") or the merits of another. See *Keter Shem Tov*, sect. 35, 133 and 260; *Likkutim Yekarim*, sect. 260.
8. Job 31:2, related to the Divine soul in man.
9. *Be'ir Elokeinu* is thus given two interpretations: In the preceding paragraph it is read in terms of our ability to serve God and overcome the *yetzer hara* "by virtue of the stirring by our God" from Above. In this paragraph it is read in terms of the admonition that our service of God must be by means of our own "stirring of the 'part' of our God within us," i.e., of our Divine soul and *yetzer tov*.

139

It is written: "The mountains will melt like wax before God." (Psalms 97:5) A verse thereafter states: "Mountains will sing together." (Psalms 98:8) How can both verses be affirmed? This may be explained as follows:

It is well-known that our sages, of blessed memory, said that "'Mountains' refers to the Fathers (Patriarchs)." (*Shemot Rabba* 15:4) They said also that "The Fathers (Patriarchs) are truly the Chariot." (*Bereishit Rabba* 47:6)[1] Now we need to understand how the Patriarchs can be the Chariot.

It is well-known that Abraham signifies the attribute of love, which is the attribute of *chessed*; Isaac signifies the attribute of fear; and Jacob signifies the attribute of *tiferet* (beauty),

---

1. The Patriarchs are the Chariot described in Ezekiel's vision (Ezekiel 1) which is, as it were, the "bearer of God": by their total submission to the Divine Will they became the vehicle and channel for Divinity on earth.

which harmonizes [love and fear].[2] Our sages, of blessed memory, said that "Israelites have three characteristics: they are compassionate, bashful, and they perform acts of kindness." (*Yevamot* 79a) These [characteristics] are the three attributes of the Patriarchs in ascending order: compassion is the attribute of Jacob; bashfulness is the attribute of Isaac, for he who is afraid of another is bashful before him; and the performance of kindness is the attribute of Abraham, i.e., *chessed*.

"God made one thing opposite the other." (Ecclesiastes 7:14)[3] These three attributes exist then likewise in the realm of impurity, referred to as "the Fathers of Impurity."[4]

The difference between the two [domains] is as follows:

In the realm of holiness the three attributes compound one another. For example, he who *loves*[5] another has *compassion*[6] for him; and if at times he is unable to provide the other's desire, he will be *bashful*[7] before him. The three thus compound one another and are as one, for holiness is earmarked by absolute unity.[8]

In the realm of impurity, however, the three attributes are separate: "all the workers of iniquity shall be *scattered*" (Psalms

---

2. *Zohar* III:301b-302a. See above, sect. 87. *Cf. Likkutim Yekarim*, sect. 129 and 280.

3. I.e., everything in the realm of holiness has a corresponding opposite in the realm of the profane and evil. *Sefer Habahir*, par. 11-12; *Zohar* I:160a; and see above, sect. 13, note 2.

4. See above, sect. 87 and 124.

5. The attribute of *Chessed*.

6. The attribute of *Tiferet*.

7. The attribute of *Gevurah*.

8. See *Zohar* III:70a and 83a. The realm of holiness thus is called "*reshut hay-achid*—the domain of the singularly one" (*Zohar* III:244a; *Tikunei Zohar* 34:69a).

92:10).[9] [There] one loves—with the alien love—one thing, but is afraid of another thing, and shows compassion for yet another thing.

This is the meaning of the verse "The mountains will melt like wax." It speaks of the "Mountains of Impurity."[10] That is why the word "together" is not mentioned here, because there is no unity among them, but only separation, as stated above. The second verse, however, speaks of the mountains that are the holy Fathers: they are an absolute unity, thus "Mountains will sing *together*."

The verse "[All the workers of iniquity] shall be scattered" alludes to the above. The evil traits in a person, Heaven forbid, are called "workers of iniquity" because they lead to iniquity itself, i.e., actual sin. The "alien traits" are not united and joined together, and that is why it says "all the workers of iniquity shall be scattered;" for they are separate and there is no unity among them. Thus it says also "the *workers* of iniquity," as opposed to "the *doers* of iniquity," implying that there is no unity even among the "workers" [that effect] iniquity.

---

9. The realm of impurity is earmarked by separation, divisiveness and pluralism. It is *"reshut harabim*—the domain of the many" (*ibid.*).
10. *Cf. Zohar* I:126a and III:208a.

140

"God, teach me Your *derech* (way), [and lead me on the *orach* (path) of uprightness . . .]." (Psalms 27:11)

It is known that *derech* refers to a trodden road and *orach* refers to an untrodden road.[1] On the latter one may sometimes stray and walk towards a place of danger. With a trodden road, however, there is no cause for straying. These two aspects relate to man as well:

---

1. See *Zohar* II:215a and III:88a.

Man has a trodden way to serve the Creator, blessed be
He. He will surely not stray from it if he follows it continuously. This refers to one who separates himself from
everything [mundane] and occupies himself day and night
with nothing but Torah [and *Mitzvot*]. He converses on
nothing beyond essential matters.

There is also another road that is not trodden, which is
called *orach*. It refers to one who sometimes converses with
others. He speaks, though, "for the sake of Heaven." That is,
he speaks of things that effect moral guidance, love of God or
fear of God, and so forth. Alternatively, he is a person who
knows how to raise words so that they ascend to holiness, as
known from a number of people.[2] Now, to engage in these
kind of conversations is surely permissible. Nonetheless, they
involve danger, for he may stray from the proper path and start
to speak also idle talk as the masses do.[3] For this reason one
must pray and petition [God], blessed be He, that He help
him when desiring to walk on this path. For without the help
of [God], blessed be He, it is easy for man to stray in that way.
Thus one must girdle his loins with prayer not to stumble into
transgression, Heaven forbid.

This, then, is the meaning of the verse, "God, teach me
Your *derech*": teach me so that I may know the trodden road,
for then I can walk it on my own. "Lead me on the *orach* [of
uprightness]" on which I may stray, i.e., I pray that "You lead

---

2. This concept is discussed in *Keter Shem Tov*, sect. 366 and 373, and see there
   also sect. 203; *Maggid Devarav Leya'akov*, sect. 98 and 175; and *Likkutim
   Yekarim*, sect. 50 and 75.

3. See *Maggid Devarav Leya'akov*, sect. 98: "The enthused person is able to sublimate simple talk (that is not of Torah or prayer) when hearing it . . . but it
   is forbidden to set out and speak it.. One is not to say, 'These are letters
   (with implicit holiness) and I shall sublimate them to their source.' Heaven
   forbid saying such, for there is a prohibition against idle talk (see *Yoma*
   19b)."

me" with the aid, help and support enabling me to go with uprightness and not crooked. For without Your help, Heaven forbid, I may stray on it, as mentioned above.

This is also alluded in the verse, "Know Him in all your ways [and He will straighten your paths (*orach*)]." (Proverbs 3:6) This means:

With regard to all trodden roads, man must himself know very well how to go and conduct himself thereon. One is capable of this knowledge and conduct. Then "He"—i.e., [God], blessed be He—"will straighten your paths (*orach*)": He will straighten for you even the untrodden roads, and aid and help you so that you will not stray.[4]

---

4. This interpretation parallels the one in R. Chaim Vital, *Likkutei Torah* on Proverbs 3:6: "'In all your ways'—i.e., in the paved road which refers to the commandments—'know Him,' that it be *lishmah* (doing them for their own sake); 'and He will straighten your paths (*orach*),' i.e., the irregular paths, as in 'crooked paths' (Judges 5:6). Though it is difficult to engage in (mundane, pleasurable activities) for the sake of Heaven, because per force man enjoys them and seeks their pleasure, He, blessed be He, will straighten them and put into your heart [to know] how to do it *lishmah*."

141

This is an important rule:

Everything in the universe contains holy sparks. Nothing is devoid of these sparks, even wood and stones.[1] There are sparks from the "breaking [of the vessels]"[2] even in all of man's deeds, even in a sin he commits.[3] What are the sparks in

---

1. R. Chaim Vital, *Eitz Chayim* 39:3; idem, *Sha'ar Hamitzvot*, Eikev. *Keter Shem Tov*, sect. 53 and 194. See above, sect. 90.
2. See above, sect. 120, note 4.
3. Man commits sins because of his desire for the pleasure derived therefrom. This desire is rooted in man's appetitive faculty which causes him to desire or loathe something and from which arise the activities of attraction and repulsion or avoidance, love and fear, anger, hate, and so forth. (Maimonides,

a sin? *Teshuvah* (repentance; return unto God)![4] When doing *teshuvah* for the sin, one elevates the sparks in it to the Supernal World. Thus it is written, *"Nosei* (He bears, i.e., forgives; lit.: "He lifts up") sin" (Exodus 34:7; *et passim*); that is, He bears and elevates the sin to on high. This is also the meaning of "my sin is too great to be borne" (Genesis 4:13), i.e., to be raised and elevated to on high.

Shemonah Perakim, ch. 1) Virtue and vice, the observance of Torah and *mitzvot* and their violations, originate there (*ibid.*, ch. 2, and his commentary on *Avot* 2:12). The appetitive faculty, therefore, is not evil. It leads to good deeds just as it may lead to sin. The various traits that it causes (love, fear etc.) are rooted in the seven attributes of the *Sefirot* (see above, sect. 87), thus in holiness. A spark of holiness is then embedded in all actions, even in sins—though the sin itself is altogether evil. (See *Keter Shem Tov*, sect. 377, and see there also sect. 82.) This allows for the possibility of *teshuvah*, of correcting the sin. (See *Keter Shem Tov*, sect. 82, 152 and 377.)

4. "*Teshuvah* is concealed within sin. *Teshuvah* is a commandment, one of the 613 precepts [of the Torah]. One is unable to do *teshuvah*, however, if there was no prior sin. Thus it follows that *teshuvah* is concealed within sin." (*Maggid Devarav Leya'akov*, sect. 217)—Obviously this does not suggest that one should sin in order to be able to observe the precept of *teshuvah*, for "he who says 'I will sin and then do *teshuvah*' is not given the opportunity to do *teshuvah*" (*Yoma* 85b). There is a form of *teshuvah* beyond repentance, called "*teshuvah ila'ah*—the supreme *teshuvah*," of returning to the higher spiritual levels from which the soul originated (*cf.* above, sect. 17, note 6), which applies to the faultless *tzadik* as well.

142

"Know what is above you (lit.: from you)." (*Avot* 2:1) This may be interpreted as follows: "Know that everything Above is all from you."[1]

---

1. This is the principle of there being a reciprocal relationship between man's conduct (in thought, speech or deed) below and the effluences or manifestations that come from Above [analogous to the concept of "In the measure with which man measures, it is meted out to him" (*Sotah* 8b), and *cf.* above,

sect. 123, note 4]. The Baal Shem Tov thus interpreted "God is your shade." (Psalms 121:5): As man's shadow copies his every movement, so does God relate to man in accordance to his actions. (*Keter Shem Tov*, Addenda, no. 60; *cf. Shenei Luchot Haberit, Sha'ar Hagadol*, p. 22a, attributing this interpretation to a *Midrash*.)

The supernal realms are affected, as it were, by man. Man's action below, therefore, effects a corresponding reaction from on high. See above, sect. 112; *Keter Shem Tov*, sect. 145 and 230; *Maggid Devarav Leya'akov*, sect. 29; the Maggid's *Or Torah*, sect. 264 and 300; and *ibid.*, Addenda, sect. 19.

143

We recite *Hodu*[1] between *Korbanot* (the recitation of the Sacrifices) and *Pesukei DeZimrah* (the Verses of Praise), as opposed to saying it within the *Pesukei DeZimrah*, for the following reason:

It is well-known that the [segment of] *Korbanot* relates to [the World of] *Asiyah*; *Pesukei DeZimrah* to [the World of] *Yetzirah*; and *Yotzer Or..* (the reading of the *Shema* and its blessings) to [the World of] *Beri'ah*.[2] This is the esoteric meaning of the *Ofanim*, the *Chayot* and the *Seraphim*.[3] The esoteric meaning of their names is as follows:

[The angels] in [the World of] *Asiyah* are called *Ofanim*, which has the connotation of a wheel. For the angels in that [world] desire and "roll" to become joined to on high. Thus

---

1. A chapter compounding verses of praise to God from I Chronicles 16 and various Psalms. In the Sefardic rite (adopted by R. Isaac Luria, and followed by the Baal Shem Tov and the Chassidic movement), this chapter is recited before the *Pesukei DeZimra* (the initial section of the formal morning-prayers).
2. R. Chaim Vital, *Peri Eitz Chayim, Sha'ar Hatefilah*, ch. 1 and 6-7.
3. These three classes of angels are of the Worlds of *Asiyah, Yetzirah* and *Beri'ah* respectively.

they also signify the category of *nefesh* (soul),[4] a term denoting addition and increase,[5] because they desire for themselves the increase of additional effluence and vitality.

The angels of the [World of] *Yetzirah* are of a higher rank. They derive their life-force from a higher source. That is why they are called *Chayot* (the "Living Ones").[6]

[[7] The angels of the [World of] *Beri'ah* are of still higher rank. They inflame themselves even more to be joined to on high. That is why they are called *Seraphim* (the "Burning Ones").[6]

Man is a miniature universe.[8] When rising from his bed in the morning, he is without any fear [of God]. As stated in the *Zohar* (III:120b), he is purified by means of [the recital of] the *Korbanot*. Thus he is in the principle of [the World of] *Asiyah*, an *Ofan* who desires and rolls to be joined unto God. How does [he do so]? By means of the *Pesukei DeZimrah*. For there is more *hitlahavut* (burning enthusiasm) in those verses than in *Korbanot*. Before he can attain great *hitlahavut*, however, he starts with lesser *hitlahavut*. That is why *Hodu* was instituted before, because it is but selected verses which are not really *Pesukei DeZimra*. Thus he is able to be in great *hitlahavut* when he gets to the *Pesukei DeZimra*, acquiring additional *chayut*

---

4. The soul-category of *nefesh* (which is of the World of *Asiyah*—*Tikunei Zohar* 22:68b; *Zohar Chadash*, Yitro:34b) relates to the *Ofanim* (*Zohar* II:94b; *Tikunei Zohar* 6:23a).

5. In Aramaic, the word *nefesh* (of the root-word *push*) means an increase and expansion, as in *Targum Onkelos* on Genesis 1:22 and Exodus 1:7.

6. The different names of the angels relate to their specific ranks (Maimonides, *Hilchot Yessodei Hatorah* 2:7).

7. The bracketed part, from here to the end of this section, was somehow omitted in the printed editions of *Tzava'at Harivash*. It is inserted here from *Likkutim Yekarim*, sect. 85.

8. Man is a microcosm which reflects the macrocosm. *Tanchuma, k:3; Avot deR. Nathan*, ch. 31; *Zohar* III:33b and 257b; *et passim*.

(life-force; vitality) because the *hitlahavut* is the vitality. With *Yotzer Or* he will have yet more *hitlahavut* and attain the level of the *Seraphim*.[9]]

---

9. See *Keter Shem Tov*, sect. 259; and *cf.* above, sect. 32, that in prayer one is to advance in gradual stages.

GLOSSARY

GLOSSARY*

Amidah—(lit. "standing" as it is a prayer that is to be recited in a standing position), also referred to as *Shemoneh Esreh* ("eighteen" benedictions); the main section of all obligatory prayers recited daily.

Assiyah*—"[World of] Action," lowest of the four "Worlds" or realms in the creative process, and on its lowest level including the physical universe.

Atzilut*—"[World of] Emanation," highest of the four "Worlds" or realms in the creative process, thus closest to actual Divinity.

Avodah tzorech gevohah—"service (or worship) for the Supernal 'need' or intent;" the service of God that focuses exclusively on the Divine intent without any mundane or personal considerations.

Beri'ah*—"[World of] Creation, the second in the four "Worlds" or realms in the creative process; abode of supreme angels and souls, and also identified as the level of the Divine Throne.

Bitul hayesh—negation of self; the state of negating or nullifying ego and all personal considerations in the consciousness of all-comprehensive Godliness.

Breaking of the vessels—see below, *Shevirat hakeilim*

Deveikut—"attachment (or cleaving) [unto God]", as ordained in the Torah, Deuteronomy 11:22; signifying all-embracing

---

*   The glossary is restricted to very brief definitions. Complex terms, marked with an asterisk, are fully explained in my *Mystical Concepts in Chassidism*.

consciousness of, and communion with, God, meditative and ecstatic, in all human (mundane) engagements just as in worship and other religious involvements.

Dinim[*]—"judgments", signifying strict or rigorous judgments decreed against humans or the world.

Gadlut—"greatness", in Chassidic terminology the sublime level of expanded consciousness and apprehension in the service and worship of God; opposite of *katnut*, see there.

Gemara—The major part of the Talmud which consists of the Talmudic traditions, discussions and rulings, based mainly on the *Mishnah*.

Hashgachah peratit—lit. "individual supervision," and (in Chassidism) referring to the Divine Providence governing every particular entity in the universe.

Hishtavut—"equanimity", the concept of total indifference to all mundane occurrences in context of the consciousness of all-encompassing reality of God.

Hitbodedut—"seclusion" from the world and people to meditate on, and commune with, the Divine.

Hitlahavut—"burning enthusiasm; fervor", the ecstatic frame of mind in the service and worship of God.

Hymns of Praise—see *Pesukei deZimra*

Katnut—"smallness", the state of constricted or restricted (limited) consciousness in the service and worship of God, as opposed to *Gadlut* (see there).

Kavanah—"direction [of the mind]", thus proper intent in, and concentration on, one's action, especially in prayer and the observance of *Mitzvot*.

Kavanot—plural of *Kavanah*, but assuming a much wider meaning in mystical context, i.e., meditating on the "mystical devotions" that relate to the words of prayer (especially the Divine Names) and to the observance of each *mitzvah*. The teachings of R. Isaac Luria (especially *Peri Eitz Chayim* and *Sha'ar Hakavanot*) offer these *kavanot*.

Kelipah (pl. *kelipot*)*—"shell(s)", the Kabbalistic term signifying the realms or entities that are evil and impure, which include all that is forbidden by the Torah.

Lishmah—"for its own sake", doing something strictly for its own sake as demanded or desired by God, without any ulterior motives of personal benefit (such as self-aggrandizement or expectation of some reward). Opposite of *shelo lishmah*, see there.

Machshavah zara (pl. *machshavot zarot*)—"alien thought(s)", any thought extraneous to one's involvement with prayer or worship, whether it be a sinful or forbidden thought or simply one inappropriate to the occasion.

Midot*—"traits; attributes". (a) The seven "lower" *Sefirot* or "emotive attributes" of God (*chessed*—kindness or love; *gevurah*—rigor or strict justice; *tiferet*—beauty or compassion; and so forth); and (b) the corresponding dispositions or character-traits in the human psyche.

Mikveh—pool for ritual immersion effecting purification from ritual or spiritual defilement.

Mitzvah (pl. *Mitzvot*)—"commandment(s)", Biblical or Rabbinic precepts; every Jew's religious obligations, and—in colloquial use—referring to good deeds in general.

Mussar—"instruction for proper behavior"; works of *mussar* offer guidance and inspiration for religious ethics and devotional instructions. In our context this relates to medieval works such as R. Bachya ibn Pakuda's *Chovot Halevovot*, and the later writings, with a mystical slant, such as *Reishit Chochmah* and *Shenei Luchot Haberit*. (This is not to be confused with the modern Mussar-movement founded in the 19th century by R. Israel Salanter.)

Nitzotz (pl. *nitzotzim* or *nitzotzot*)[*]—"spark(s)". Jewish mysticism teaches that every entity (good or evil) contains "holy sparks" of Divinity which constitute the very vitality or sustaining force of each. These sparks "fell" or descended from Above with the *shevirat hakeilim*. It is man's task to "correct"— "free" or extricate—these sparks by relating to every thing in its Divinely intended context: good or permissible things become sublimated to holiness by using them properly ("active correction"); evil or forbidden things are nullified when their sparks are extricated by relating to them as prescribed ("passive correction" by abstention or discardment).

Peniyah (pl. *peniyot*)—"ulterior motive(s)" of personal gain or satisfaction.

Pesukei Dezimrah—"verses of praise", a collection of Biblical hymns and psalms recited daily at the beginning of the morning-prayers, thus first praising God before submitting our personal petitions.

Sefirah (pl. *Sefirot*)[*]—term denoting the ten Divine attributes or emanations through which God manifests Himself in both the creation and sustenance of all beings. These include the seven *Midot* (see above) and the higher *Sefirot* of *Keter, Chochmah* and *Binah* (and in other schemes *Chochmah, Binah* and *Da'at*).

Shechinah—"Indwelling", the Divine Presence or Immanence in creation, as distinguished from the Divine Transcendence (usually represented by the term *Hakadosh baruch Hu*—the

Holy One, blessed is He). This term is in feminine gender, while the transcendent aspect is in male gender.

Shelo lishmah—"not for its own sake", the opposite of *lishmah* (see there), which manifests itself in the omission of the proper *kavanah* or intent, or—in the crudest sense—in the commission of being guided by ulterior motives.

Shema—"Hear", the first word and title of the Biblical passages of Deuteronomy 6:4-9, 11:13-21, and Numbers 15:37-41, which are to be recited every day and every night.

Shevirat hakeilim[*]—"breaking of the vessels", a central concept in Kabbalistic cosmogony which accounts for the multiplicity, and the presence of evil, in the universe, by scattering the "sparks" from the fragmentation of the "vessels" throughout creation.

Shulchan Aruch—title of the standard code of Jewish law, compiled by R. Joseph Karo.

Sidur—lit. "order"; term for prayer-book.

Sitra achara[*]—"the other side", as opposed to the side of holiness; a general term for evil, compounding anything that is separated from, or opposed to, Godliness.

Sparks—see *nitzotz*.

Teshuvah—"return" to God. In the narrow sense, the act of repentance from all sins of omission or commission. In the wider sense, returning to God in the sense of a continuously progressive advance to Godliness, thus applying to the non-sinner (the *tzadik*) no less than to the sinner.

Tikun chatzot—"order of midnight-service"; midnight-vigil focused on mourning the destruction of the Holy Temple in Jerusalem and the exile of the Jewish people, but also containing an order of Torah-study.

Tzadik (pl. **tzadikim**)—"the righteous"; in the general sense any righteous (pious) person, but in Chassidic context referring more specifically to extra-ordinary saints.

Tzimtzum[*]—"contraction; concealment"; the Kabbalistic concept of the contraction and concealment of the consuming intensity of the Divine "light" through a series of stages (e.g., the four "Worlds" of *Atzilut, Beri'ah, Yetzirah* and *Assiyah*), that makes it possible for finite and material substances to come about.

Tzorech gevohah—see above, *avodah tzorech gevohah*.

World—when this term appears qualified in our text (e.g., "World of *Atzilut*," or "World of Thought") it refers to the relevant *spiritual* realm or level.

Yetzer hara—"evil impulse", the human inclination or impulse to sin by omission or commission, rooted in the physical nature and "animal soul" of man.

Yetzer hatov—"good impulse", the human inclination or impulse to do good, rooted in the spiritual nature (Divine soul) of man.

Yetzirah[*]—"[World of] Formation", the third of the four "worlds" or realms in the creative process; abode of a lower class of angels than those in *Beri'ah*.

Yichudim—"unifications", acts effecting unifications in the spiritual realms by meditating on the relevant *kavanot* (see there).

Zerizut—"alacrity", performing obligations with alacrity and zeal.

Ze'eyr anpin[*]—"small image (or visage)"; Kabbalistic term for the compound of the first six *midot* (*chessed* to *yessod*), central to Kabbalistic cosmogony.

BIBLIOGRAPHY

BIBLIOGRAPHY

A. Chassidic Works

ARVEI NACHAL, R. David Shelomoh Eibeshitz, Warsaw [n.d.]

BEN PORAT YOSSEF, R. Ya'akov Yossef of Polnoy, New York 1954

BE'URIM BETZAVA'AT HARIVASH, R. Menachem M. Schneerson of Lubavitch, ed. J. I. Schochet; 2nd ed., Kehot: Brooklyn NY 1985

DARKEI YESHARIM, attributed to R. Menachem Mendel of Prezemishlan (Przemysl), Przemysl 1890; with title HANHAGOT YESHAROT, Warsaw 1913

DEGEL MACHANEH EPHRAYIM, R. Mosheh Chayim Ephrayim of Sudylkov, Jerusalem 1963

DERECH PIKUDECHA, R. Tzvi Elimelech of Dinov, Lemberg 1921

HANHAGOT YESHAROT, see DARKEI YESHARIM

IGROT KODESH—ADMUR HAZAKEN, Letters by R. Schneur Zalman of Liadi, 2 vol., Brooklyn NY 1980-1993

KEDUSHAT LEVI, R. Levi Yitzchak of Berdichev, Jerusalem 1964

KETER SHEM TOV, Anthology of teachings of the Baal Shem Tov compiled by R. Aaron of Apt; ed. Kehot, 4th edition, Brooklyn NY 1987

LIKKUTEI AMARIM, Anthology of teachings of the Maggid of Mezhirech, attributed to R. Menachem Mendel of Vitebsk, Brooklyn NY 1962

LIKKUTIM YEKARIM, Anthology of teachings of the Baal Shem Tov, the Maggid of Mezhirech, and (four of) R. Yechiel Michel of Zloczov, Yeshivat Toldot Aharon: Jerusalem 1974

MAGGID DEVARAV LEYA'AKOV, Anthology of teachings of the Maggid of Mezhirech; ed. Kehot, 3rd edition, Brooklyn NY 1980

ME'OR EINAYIM, R. Menachem Nachum of Czernobyl, Brooklyn NY 1975

OR HA'EMET, Anthology of teachings of the Maggid of Mezhirech, Brooklyn NY 1960

OR HAME'IR, R. Ze'ev Wolf of Zhitomir, Lemberg 1850

OR TORAH, Anthology of teachings of the Maggid of Mezhirech; ed. Kehot, 3rd edition, Brooklyn NY 1980

TANYA, R. Schneur Zalman of Liadi, Brooklyn NY 1965

TOLDOT YA'AKOV YOSSEF, R. Ya'akov Yossef of Polnoy, Jerusalem 1960

TORAT HAMAGGID MIMEZHIRECH, ed. Y. Klapholtz, Tel Aviv 1969

TZAFNAT PANE'ACH, R. Ya'akov Yossef of Polnoy, Brooklyn NY 1954

YOSHER DIVREI EMET, included in LIKKUTIM YEKARIM, see there.

B. Other Sources

BEIT ELOKIM, R. Mosheh of Torani, Warsaw 1831

CHAREIDIM, R. Eleazar Azkari, Jerusalem 1958

CHIBUR HATESHUVAH, R. Menachem Me'iri, Jerusalem 1976

DERECH CHAYIM, R. Judah Loewe, London 1960

EITZ CHAYIM, R. Chaim Vital, ed. Warsaw 1891, [Israel] 1975

HA'EMUNAH VEHABITACHON, R. Mosheh Nachmanides, in KITVEI RAMBAN, ed. Chavel, Jerusalem 1963

KAD HAKEMACH, R. Bachya ben Asher, New York 1960

MENORAT HAMA'OR, R. Israel ibn Al-Nakawa, New York 1929-32

NAGGID UMETZAVEH, R. Ya'akov Chaim Tzemach, [Israel, n.d.]

OR HACHAMAH, R. Abraham Azulay, Przemysl 1896

PERI EITZ CHAYIM, R. Chaim Vital, ed. R. Abraham Brandwein, Jerusalem 1980

REISHIT CHOCHMAH, R. Elijah de Vidas, Amsterdam 1708

SEFER CHASSIDIM, ed. R. Margolius, Jerusalem 1957

SHENEI LUCHOT HABERIT, R. Isaiah Horowitz, ed. Warsaw, Jerusalem 1963

SIDDUR HA'ARI, R.Shabtay of Rashkov, [Israel, n.d.]

TIFERET YISRAEL, R. Judah Loewe, New York NY 1969

INDEX OF BIBLICAL AND
RABBINIC QUOTATIONS IN TEXT

INDEX OF BIBLICAL AND RABBINIC QUOTATIONS IN TEXT*

BIBLE

---

*   All references are to the sections in our text. For example, "Genesis 3:6...5" means that this verse is cited in section 5.

TALMUD

MIDRASHIM

INDEX OF SUBJE

INDEX OF SUBJECTS*

APPENDIX

APPENDIX

There are currently three principal editions of R. Dov Ber of Mezhirech's *Maggid Devarav Laya'akov:* 1) ed. Kehot (New York); 2) ed. Toldot Aharon (Jerusalem); and 3) ed. Schatz-Uffenheimer (Jerusalem). The major difference between them is the editors' division (thus numbering) of the contents. All references in this work are to ed. Kehot. The following table offers the equivalent numberings in the other editions. (Note that ed. Schatz-Uffenheimer somehow skipped nos. 11 and 136 in its numberings.)

K	TA	SU		K	TA	SU
1	1	1		22	26	17
2	2	1		23	27	18
3	2	1		24	28	19
4	3	2		25	29	20
5	4-5	3-4		26	30	21
6	6-7	5		27	31	22
7	8	6		28	32	23
8	9	7		29	33	24
9	10	8		30	34	25
10	11-2	8		31	35	25
11	11-2	9-10		32	35	25
12	13-4	12		33	36	25
13	15-6	13		34	37	25
14	17-8	14		35	38	25
15	19-20	14		36	39	26
16	21	14		37	40	26
17	22	14		38	41	26
18	23	15		39	42	26
19	23	15		40	43	27
20	23	15		41	44	28
21	24-5	16		42	45	28

K	TA	SU	K	TA	SU
43	46	28	82	93	53
44	47	28	83	94	54
45	48-50	28	84	95	55
46	51	29	85	95	55
47	52-3	29	86	96	56
48	54	30	87	97	57
49	55-7	31	88	98	58
50	58-62	31	89	99	59
51	63-4	31	90	100	60
52	65	31	91	100	60
53	66	32	92	101	61
54	66-8	32	93	102	62
55	69	32	94	103	63
56	70	34	95	104	63
57	71	35	96	105	64
58	71	34-35	97	106	65
59	72	36	98	107	66
60	73	36	99	108	67
61	74	37	100	109	68
62	75	38	101	110	69
63	76	38	102	111	70
64	77	39	103	112	71
65	78	40	104	113-5	71
66	79	40	105	116	72
67	80	41	106	117	73
68	80	41	107	118	74
69	81	42	108	119-120	75-6
70	82	43	109	121	77
71	83	44	110	122	78
72	84	45	111	123	79
73	84	45	112	123	79
74	85	46	113	124	80
75	86	47	114	125	81
76	87	48	115	126	82
77	88	49	116	126	82
78	89	50	117	127	82
79	90-1	51	118	128	83
80	91	51	119	129	84
81	92	52	120	130	85

K	TA	SU
121	[130]	85
122	131	86
123	132	87
124	133	88
125	134	89
126	135	90
127	136	91
128	137	92
129	138	93
130	139	94
131	140	95
132	140	95
133	141	96
134	142	97
135	143-4	98
136	145	99
137	146	100
138	146	100
139	147	101
140	148	102
141	149	103
142	150	104
143	151	105
144	152	105
145	153	105
146	154	106
147	155	107
148	156	107
149	157	108
150	158	109
151	159	110
152	160	111
153	161	112
154	162	113
155	163	113
156	164	114
157	165	115
158	166	116
159	167	117

K	TA	SU
160	168	118
161	169	119
162	170	120
163	171	121
164	172	122
165	185	142
166	173	123
167	174	124
168	175	125
169	175	125
170	176	126
171	176	126
172	177	127
173	178	128
174	179	129
175	180	130
176	181	131
177	182	132
178	183	133
179	184	134-5
180	186	137
181	187	137
182	188	138
183	189	139
184	190	140
185	191	141
186	193	143
187	194	143
188	195-6	144
189	197	145
190	198-200	146
191	201	146
192	202	147
193	203	148
194	204	149
195	205	149
196	206	150
197	207	151
198	208	151

K	TA	SU	K	TA	SU
199	209	151	237	250	181
200	210	152	238	251	182
201	211	152	239	252	183
202	212	153	240	253	184
203	213	154	241	254	185
204	214	155	242	255	186
205	215	156	243	256	187
206	216	157	244	257	188
207	217	158	245	258	189
208	218	159	246	259	189
209	219	160	247	258	189
210	219	160	248	258	189
211	220	161	249	260	190
212	221	161	250	261	191
213	222-4	161	251	262	192
214	225	161	252	262	192
215	226	161	253	262	192
216	227	162	254	263	193
217	228	163	255	263	193
218	229	164	256	264	194
219	230-1	165-6	257	265	195
220	232	167	258	266	196
221	233	168	259	267	197
222	234	168	260	268	198
223	235-6	168	261	269	199
224	237	169	262	270	200
225	237	170	263	271	201
226	238	171	264	272	202
227	239	172	265	273	203
228	240-2	173	266	274	204
229	243	174	267	275	205
230	244	175	268	276	206
231	245	176	269	277	207
232	246	177	270	278	208
233	247	178	271	278	208
234	248	179	272	278	208
235	248	179	273	278	208
236	249	180	274	279	209

לזכות

יעקב עמנואל בן שרה שאשע
רחל בת יטלא אסתר

יהודית אוריה בת רחל
אלחנן אביגדור בן פריידא זיסל
ובניהם לוי יצחק, אהרן יחזקאל, דוב יהודה,
אברהם, ברוך שלום, חוה מושקא

יצחק יהונתן בן רחל
חנה בת טשערנא רייזל
ובניהם מרדכי יאיר, דוב יהודה, מנחם מענדל

חנה שרון בת רחל
יוסף בנימין בן רחל
ובניהם אברהם ברוך, מנחם מענדל,
רפאל משה, חיה מושקא

ישראל עובדיה בן רחל
נחמה דינה בת פייגא צביה

ה' עליהם יחיו
לאריכות ימים ושנים טובות ובריאות
זכות הבעל שם טוב והרב המגיד
תגן עליהם, בתוך כלל ישראל, לברכה ולהצלחה
בכל ענייניהם הפרטיים והכלליים בגשמיות
וברוחניות גם יחד